GIRLS
MAKE
MOVIES

GIRLS MAKE MOVIES

A FOLLOW-YOUR-OWN-PATH GUIDE FOR ASPIRING YOUNG FILMMAKERS

MALLORY O'MEARA

Illustrated by
JEN VAUGHN

RP|KIDS
PHILADELPHIA

Running Press Kids
Hachette Book Group
1290 Avenue of the Americas, New York, NY 10104
www.runningpress.com/rpkids
@RP_Kids

Printed in China

First Edition: May 2023

Published by Running Press Kids, an imprint of Perseus Books, LLC,
a subsidiary of Hachette Book Group, Inc. The Running Press Kids name
and logo are trademarks of the Hachette Book Group.

The Hachette Speakers Bureau provides a wide range of authors for speaking events.
To find out more, go to www.hachettespeakersbureau.com or call (866) 376-6591.

The publisher is not responsible for websites (or their content)
that are not owned by the publisher.

Print book cover and interior design by Frances J. Soo Ping Chow.

Library of Congress Control Number: 2022937067

ISBNs: 978-0-7624-7898-9 (hardcover), 978-0-7624-7899-6 (ebook)

1010

10 9 8 7 6 5 4 3 2 1

FOR ALL THE WOMEN IN FILM.
NEVER STOP.

GIRLS MAKE MOVIES

INTRODUCTION

MOVIES ARE AWESOME.

I've always loved movies, ever since I was a little kid. What I didn't know then was that making movies is also awesome, maybe even *more* awesome than watching them.

When I was little, I thought that movies were made with just actors, a director, and a camera. I didn't realize that every single thing you see on screen—every single thing you *hear*, every single thing you *feel* when you're watching—was carefully crafted by a huge group of people. Movies take a lot of work, time, and, most importantly, a ton of cooperation and imagination.

What I also didn't realize was that *girls* make movies. Lots and lots of girls. When I got older and started making movies, I was so excited to learn about all the different kinds of jobs you can have in the movie business. Being an actor or a director is fantastic, but there's more to it. Much more. There are a lot of women who are actors and directors, of course, but those jobs in between? Women do those, too.

If I had known about all the different ways you can be involved in a movie when I was a kid, I would have started making them way sooner. Personally, I was never very interested in being an actor, because being in front of a camera makes me nervous. What I do love, however, is writing movies. I love producing them. I love organizing things and making really cool things with my friends.

I really wish I could go back in time and tell all this stuff to myself. Since time machines don't exist yet, I did the next best thing: I wrote this book so that all the girls who are growing up *now* can learn it.

Did you know that the first movie ever directed by a woman came out way back in 1896? They didn't even have peanut M&Ms and Cherry Coke (the best movie snacks) back then. The director's name was Alice Guy-Blaché and her movie was the very first narrative film—that is, a movie with a story—ever made. It was in French and called *La fée aux choux*, which in English is "The fairy of the cabbages." A lady made the first movie *ever*. And it was about a fairy. How cool is that?

The world needs more girls making movies. Why? Because a world without movies made by girls would be a sad place. Girls making stuff is how you get movies like *Frozen*, *A Wrinkle in Time*, and *Brave*. What would we all do without *Frozen*? What would we sing at karaoke?!

Girls have been making movies for more than 120 years, and nowadays, there are more girls making movies than ever before. Happy movies, sad movies, scary movies, romantic movies. Movies with monsters, movies with kissing, even movies about kissing monsters. Girls can do anything they want in the world of making movies, and so can you.

It's important to know all this stuff because what you can see, you can be. You—yes, you—can be a director, or a writer, or a producer. Maybe you want to be a costume designer or a special effects artist. Or maybe you'd rather be a cinematographer, a foley artist, or a gaffer. Of course, those sound like fun jobs, but what do women in those roles actually *do*? Well, you're about to find out.

Girls Make Movies will teach you what you need to know about how to make a movie, and about all the different women who work behind, and in front of, the camera. What do you do? What tools do you need? How do you start? Don't worry, all those questions and more will be answered.

First, there are four stages to making a movie: development, pre-production, production, and post-production. So this book is also broken up into four sections. Each stage (and section) is exciting and challenging in its own way. Development involves the planning for the movie and needs some top-notch organization. Pre-production is all the preparation, getting everything from the sets to the actors ready. There will be a whole lot of creativity in this stage. Production is when you actually shoot the movie, which requires serious cooperation. Finally, post-production is when you edit all the footage and make everything look and sound fantastic. Patience is the name of the game in this last stage.

In each section, you're going to learn what happens during each stage, why it's important, and all the different roles and jobs involved. Then, by the end of this book, you'll be ready to start filming cool stuff with your friends.

I hope you have as much fun making movies as I do.

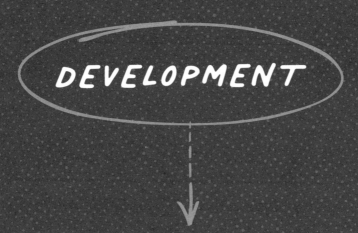

DEVELOPMENT

This is the first stage of making a movie. Development is when the plan for a movie is created. It's the stage when all the parts that form the foundation of a movie are brought together, such as the story, the overall look, and how much everything is going to cost. There are always a lot of ideas, and there are lots of lists to keep track of everything. Tons of organizing and writing and planning happens at this stage. But, because it's about making a movie, it is *fun* organizing and writing and planning. Yes, that might sound suspicious, but it is the truth. We promise.

DAY
ONE

DAWN OF THE ZOMBIE MOVIE

MOVIES START, LIKE ALL GOOD THINGS, WITH AN IDEA. The first thing we need to do is turn that idea into a *screenplay*. A screenplay is like a map for a movie, and the woman who creates it is called a *screenwriter*.

> ALTHOUGH WE ARE TALKING ABOUT MOVIES, SCREENWRITING INCLUDES ANY TYPE OF WRITING FOR THE SCREEN, WHETHER IT IS FOR MOVIES OR TELEVISION, FICTIONAL FILMS, OR DOCUMENTARIES.

Even if you already have a rough idea of what happens during the movie's plot, you need a lot more information to make it. A screenplay not only plans what the movie is about, but it also provides the actors' lines (a.k.a. the *dialogue*), as well as directions for their action and important information about how the movie is going to be made. How long will the movie be? What are the characters like? How many actors are needed? Where does the movie take place? A good screenwriter answers all these questions, and more, in her screenplay.

A screenwriter might work alone, or she might have a writing partner or even be part of a writing team. Being part of a writing partnership or team means you are a *cowriter*. For example, the movie *Bend It Like Beckham* was cowritten by Gurinder Chadha—she also codirected it!

Some screenwriters create screenplays from original ideas, like Melissa Mathison did with *E.T.: The Extra-Terrestrial*. Other screenwriters *adapt* their screenplays. Adapting a screenplay means taking a book—or an already existing story—and turning it into a movie. Many movies start as adaptations from books, video games, and even amusement park rides, like *Pirates of the Caribbean* and *Jungle Cruise*. They might be sequels to or reboots of existing movies.

> THAT'S WHY THERE ARE TWO SCREENWRITING CATEGORIES AT THE OSCARS:
> BEST ORIGINAL SCREENPLAY AND BEST ADAPTED SCREENPLAY!

A screenplay can go through many drafts before it reaches its final form. Depending on the movie, this process can take weeks, months, or sometimes even years. Good things take time!

ℓℓℓℓℓℓℓℓ

Okay, so let's say there's a screenwriter who wants to write an original screenplay about . . . zombies. Even better, teenagers fighting zombies. Her screenplay will be called *Sasha Versus Zombies*, about a teenage girl—a YouTube makeup star called Sasha Screams, to be more precise—and her friends who survive an undead invasion in their small town by disguising themselves as zombies with Sasha's special effects makeup.

Now that the screenwriter has her main characters and a basic idea of the plot, she's off to the races and can begin writing the screenplay. Screenwriters need to write in a specific format so that all the information is easy to read and find by other people, so unfortunately, *Sasha Versus Zombies* can't start out with "Once upon a time . . ." If the screenwriter were just writing a fiction story, it would look like this:

> **Sasha woke up in her sunlit bedroom. She got up to look out the window and muttered, "Another beautiful day in Boringville."**

But in a screenplay, or *script*, it would look like this:

> *INT. SASHA'S BEDROOM—MORNING*
>
> *Sasha wakes up in her bed. She gets up to look out the window.*
>
> > *SASHA*
> > *Another beautiful day in Boringville.*

The reason for this weird format is to show whether a scene is inside or outside, what location or set it's in, and also what time of day it is.

> THAT'S WHAT INT. STANDS FOR, INTERIOR.
> IT WOULD BE EXT. IF IT WAS SET OUTSIDE, FOR EXTERIOR.

When you read this scene, you know that it's shot inside Sasha's bedroom and it's morning. These are really important details to know when filming a scene.

The general rule of screenwriting for movies is that one page is roughly equal to one minute of screentime. With this format, anyone can tell how long a movie is going to be by the length of the screenplay. If *Sasha Versus Zombies* ends up at ninety pages, it will be about an hour and a half long.

A screenwriter includes only a small amount of description in her screenplays. Instead of writing:

> *Sasha excavates herself from the warm depths of her bedding. Her quilt is fluffy and stitched with huge sunflowers, like a soft field of petals. She pulls back the quilt and covers her mouth while she yawns, her golden nail polish sparkling in the early morning sun.*

She can just write:

> *Sasha sits up in bed and yawns.*

She doesn't have to worry about costume details for Sasha, or what her bedroom is going to look like, or how the camera is going to move in the scene. The director, with the help of other women on the team, will make those decisions. So, the screenwriter gets to focus on the story, the dialogue, and the action.

Does this seem fun? Does becoming a screenwriter sound like a job for you? Learning how to write a screenplay is easy, and to become a screenwriter, all you need is a cool story idea and access to a computer at home, school, or your local library. If you want to learn more about how to write and format a screenplay, then you can look at the resources page at the end of this book (132) and find a list of free online resources that will help.

Okay, now that we have a finished screenplay, we are ready to move on to the next step in making a movie, and the fun can really begin.

DAY SEVEN

INVASION OF THE MOVIE SNATCHERS

WHEN THE SCREENWRITER FINISHES THE SCREENPLAY, SHE SENDS it off to a team who will bring the story to life. They'll take the information and outline she has provided in her script and run with it.

The first person to read the screenplay will be the *producer*. She has one of the most important roles on a film crew and is responsible for getting the movie made. A movie producer is sort of like the manager of the movie, and they have a lot of responsibility. Producers are responsible for the *budget*, or how much everything is going to cost and how much everyone on the team is going to get paid; they are also in charge of the movie's schedule and making sure everything happens on time. They bring the movie's crew together and hire each person, plus make sure everyone is doing their jobs the right way, at the right time. A producer is one of the only people on a movie, besides the director, who's involved from the very beginning to the very end.

> PRODUCER NINA JACOBSON HAS WORKED ON MOVIES LIKE THE HUNGER GAMES AND CRAZY RICH ASIANS! IN 2012, SHE TOLD COLLIDER THAT MAKING SUCCESSFUL MOVIES IS ABOUT MAKING SOMETHING THAT AUDIENCES "LIKE AND WANT TO SEE MORE OF" AND THAT PRODUCING THE HUNGER GAMES MOVIES WAS ALL ABOUT FOCUSING ON MAKING THE BEST MOVIE SHE COULD.

Movie producing is the perfect job if you like being in charge, but it also comes with a ton of responsibility. You've got to be really good at communicating, being organized, and solving problems. But if that all sounds like fun to you, then being a producer will be a blast. It's exciting to see a project you put together turn into a finished film.

While it sounds like a difficult job, it is not difficult to learn how to be a producer, and you can start by planning a movie in your own backyard. If you, or one of your friends or family members, wants to make a movie, then you organize how, when, and where the movie will happen. And, congratulations, you're a producer!

Alright, so the producer gets the *Sasha Versus Zombies* script from the screenwriter, which is about Sasha, a sixteen-year-old who lives in a small town outside of Los Angeles. Sasha and her three best friends—Maddie, KC, and Charlie—are all getting ready to shoot a new gory makeup video for Sasha's YouTube channel when they notice some people shambling down the street . . . and they don't look so good. Sasha's parents are on vacation, so the foursome needs to figure out what to do all by themselves. After the group takes down one zombie in the backyard, Sasha has an idea. Using her makeup skills, she'll disguise the group as undead, so they can all escape the oncoming horde and get to the high school, where the town is gathering for safety.

The producer absolutely freaking loves the script. Now that the producer has a great story, she approves it and next needs to find someone to direct it.

ееееееее

If a movie is a ship, then the *director* is the captain. She's the person who is at the helm of the project and makes the creative decisions about how the movie is going to look. Not only does the director creatively guide the movie, she also is responsible for overseeing and working with the rest of the crew to create it.

A film crew is made up of many departments, such as lighting, sets, and makeup, and each department has a person who supervises it, known as the department head. Each of these department heads are responsible for a single aspect or element of the movie, and the director oversees all the department heads. She helps coordinate all the ideas and creative choices everyone working on the movie makes, from the cameras to the costumes.

The director has a pretty big range of responsibilities because there are lots of choices to make and details to keep track of. How are the actors doing? Does the set look okay? Did the costumes turn out alright? She's the one calling all the shots.

Are you interested in directing something? A director can start at any age and with any level of experience or learning. No matter your background, all you need is a plan to get started and some sort of camera—even a smartphone.

PANDORA DIRECTOR BREA GRANT SAYS, "DIRECTING IS A TON OF FUN. AS A KID, I ALWAYS WANTED TO BE AN ACTRESS BECAUSE I WOULD LOOK AT THE SCREEN AND SAY, 'WELL, WHO DID THIS? I GUESS IT'S THE ACTORS!' I DIDN'T KNOW ANYTHING ELSE. ONCE I GOT OLDER AND REALIZED THERE WAS THIS WHOLE JOB WHERE YOU COULD MAKE MOVIES HAPPEN, THEN I GOT INTERESTED IN THAT. MY FATHER ALWAYS SAID I WAS GOING TO GROW UP AND BE A WARDEN BECAUSE I'M SO BOSSY AND STUBBORN. AND I FOUND THE NEXT BEST JOB WAS MAKING MOVIES!"

The producer is the person who finds and hires the director. Finding the perfect match for the screenplay is extremely important. She might already have someone in mind when she reads the script, or she might take a bunch of meetings with potential directors. The producer will consider questions like, Has this director worked on a movie like this before? What sort of style and artistic eye does this director have? And, of course, would this director be interested in this story, and does she have a strong vision for what the movie will be?

Deciding which director to pair with the script has a huge effect on the movie. It's one of the biggest choices a producer can make. After all, it will be the director's vision and creative ideas that guide the whole movie-making process.

If the producer was interested in some high-octane action, she might consider Cathy Yan, director of *Birds of Prey: And the Fantabulous Emancipation of One Harley Quinn*. Or if she was interested in a more character-driven story, she might consider Ava DuVernay, director of *A Wrinkle in Time*. One director could pitch the producer on a version of *Sasha Versus Zombies* that is dark and scary, really leaning into the zombies and horror parts of the story. Another director could pitch the producer on a version that's fun and silly, more *Shaun of the Dead* than *28 Days Later*.

Like the producer, a director is involved in the entire process and is one of the few people who are part of the team from the very beginnings of development all the way to the final version. These two women are the main forces driving the movie forward, with the producer overseeing all the organizational tasks of the film and the director handling all the creative decisions.

After having a bunch of meetings and hearing ideas from various directors, the producer will choose the one she thinks is the right fit for *Sasha Versus Zombies*. Then, once the director is hired and joins the team, the producer meets with the director and the screenwriter together. During these meetings, they can talk about the movie and the director's vision and ideas, so this way, if the director thinks any changes should be made to the script, the screenwriter can work on them before the movie is developed any further.

Does the development stage mostly involve a lot of meetings? Yes. Are they fun meetings because the producer, director, and writer are planning a movie? Also yes.

The screenwriter, producer, and director all have the most responsibility in shaping the film, and once they're all on board, projects like *Sasha Versus Zombies* can go forward and start becoming less screenplay-like and more movie-like.

Now that the core team is established, they can move to the next stage of movie-making, which is known as pre-production. Or, if they think *Sasha Versus Zombies* needs a bit more development, they can bring someone else onto the team to help them out.

Sometimes, it helps to know ahead of time how some of the sets and characters are going to look before the film moves to pre-production, so the team asks a special type of film artist to create illustrations from the director's ideas for sets and characters. This means development will take a little longer but there will be more help with planning and bringing the director's vision to life.

What do you want to do next?

A. Figure out how the movie is going to look!

Flip to the next page.

B. Move to the next moviemaking stage!

Flip to page 13 and learn about pre-production.

DAY
FOURTEEN

THE ARTIST
WITH ALL THE GIFTS

FANTASY, SCIENCE FICTION, AND HORROR MOVIES OFTEN USE
imaginative elements like unicorns, spaceships, or zombies. Maybe even zombie
unicorns, or zombie unicorns on a spaceship. Whatever the case may be, it's
helpful for the team to decide what those specific elements are going to look like early
in a movie's development.

Often, paintings and drawings of special characters, monsters, sets, and scenes are
made to help the team visualize and discuss what materials and people are needed to
make them. They also give the whole film crew a better idea of what the director wants
the movie to look like. These paintings, drawings, sculptures, and other pieces of art
are called *concept art*, and the person who makes them is called a *concept artist*.

The goal of concept art is to help explain or communicate ideas, for the director to
show to other people working on the movie to share what she envisions. If the concept
artist is successful, that piece of art will give the other people working on the movie a
good sense of what that scene is supposed to look like and how it's supposed to feel,
whether that is scary, exciting, or romantic.

CONCEPT ARTIST KARLA ORTIZ HELPED DEVELOP THE WAY CHARACTERS LOOK IN
MARVEL MOVIES LIKE BLACK PANTHER, DOCTOR STRANGE, AND THOR: RAGNAROK. SHE
ILLUSTRATED SHURI FLYING THROUGH THE AIR TO FIGHT AN ENEMY, THOR STANDING
IN HIS COOL SUPERHERO COSTUME, AND DOCTOR STRANGE FLOATING DOWN FROM ABOVE
WITH HIS BIG, RED CAPE. THESE PIECES HELPED THE WHOLE FILMMAKING TEAM BEHIND
THOSE MOVIES BRING THOSE COSTUMES, CHARACTERS, AND SCENES TO LIFE.

To get started, the concept artist will create sketches inspired by what she reads
in the screenplay and hears from the director. Sometimes, the work she needs to do is
simple, such as a single character standing on an otherwise blank page. Other times,
the filmmakers need something more elaborate, like a whole scene that depicts a lot of
actions and many different characters. It all depends on the project!

For a film like *Sasha Versus Zombies*, the director wants some zombie concept art, so she meets up with the concept artist to talk about what kind of zombies she likes from different movies or comics. The two then think about what might be best for the film.

Maybe the zombies still look fresh, so they are still held together and not too scary. Maybe it would be more fun if they're really far gone, all rotten and gloopy. But, if the zombies are going to be chasing teens around Sasha's town, they probably need to still look sort of like people and not be *too* gross. It's hard to chase after someone when your arms are rotting off, after all. Zombies that can't chase you aren't very scary.

After lots of good discussion with the director, the *Sasha Versus Zombies* concept artist gets to work creating a bunch of sketches of different versions of zombie scenes from the screenplay. Then the director chooses the one—maybe more than one—that best matches her vision for the film, like a sketch of zombies banging on the windows of a high school building. The zombies in the illustration wouldn't be too rotten but would still be scary because they look strong enough to bust down a door. The concept artist also creates a few other pieces that depict Sasha's idyllic little town . . . but with serious undead creepiness taking over. Which is just like what the director saw in her head when she read the script. Perfect!

With a visual direction in mind, the concept artist creates even more art of different characters and scenes, then sends them on to the director and producer to be reviewed and approved.

A. Now that the concept art is figured out,

   you can move to the next stage of making a film.

B. Head into pre-production by flipping to the next page!

PRE-PRODUCTION

This is the stage when the movie really starts to pick up steam and move forward on its journey. During development, everything is planned out for the movie. So, the next stage, pre-production, is when the producer gathers the people and things she needs to put those plans in action. (That's why you always need a plan.)

Pre-production is when all the important visual elements are either made, like costumes, sets, and props, or found, like the locations and the actors. The roadmap for pre-production is the screenplay, which will guide the filmmaking team as they gather everything they need to shoot the movie.

This stage is a lot of fun and full of creativity, but it's important, too, because the decisions made during this stage will make a big difference in how the movie is shot and filmed.

THE NIGHTMARE
BEFORE PRODUCTION

SCREENPLAY? *CHECK.* PRODUCER? *CHECK.* DIRECTOR? *CHECK.*
So far, so good.

While the development of a movie can take a really long time, the pre-production stage is a much quicker process. Pre-production usually takes weeks or months, instead of months or years. It's like how it might take months to think up a good idea for Halloween but only a few days to make the actual costume. With the screenplay finished and the creative direction decided on during development, it takes less time than you'd think to make what is needed to bring that screenplay to life.

When a movie enters pre-production, one of the first things that happens is the producer creates a *script breakdown.* This is a big list of everything that is needed, from either a creative or technical standpoint, for each scene in a movie. It breaks down, page by page, all of the zillion elements, like actors, location, props, and costumes, that are required. The script breakdown is one of the key tools used in pre-production, and it helps all the members on a film's crew figure out what they need to do or make.

Even a scene that seems simple, like Sasha and her three friends running down the street from some zombies, can require a lot of elements. For example, for this scene the script breakdown would include:

- Four actors to play Sasha and her friends
- Costume, shoes, hair, and makeup for each actor
- Several zombie actors or computer-generated zombies
- Costumes, hair, and makeup for the zombie actors
- Lighting
- Cameras to shoot the scene
- Sound equipment
- A neighborhood location for it all to take place

That's a lot of stuff for just one scene! So this is why it's important to find a very organized producer to keep track of everything.

eeeeeee

While you probably were already a little familiar with what a director does, you might not know about all the other people on a film crew who have a huge impact on the movie. One of the most important crew members to find and hire early in the pre-production process is a *director of photography.*

A DP is responsible for filming and capturing the look of the movie as well as for the crew working with all the camera equipment, like the camera lenses and the lighting. She works very closely with the director to make sure the camera is filming all the shots in the right way.

Lots of DPs get into this type of work because they're fascinated with photography. They're good at considering color and light and shadow and mood, especially how they all work together. Being a DP is a job that combines artistry with a lot of cool technology. If you're interested in cameras, if you're always trying to pick out the *perfect* Instagram filter, and you love movies, then being a DP might be the perfect job for you.

IF YOU NOTICED THE BEAUTIFUL SHOTS IN THE 2019 FILM *THE SUN IS ALSO A STAR,* THEN YOU SHOULD KNOW THAT THEY WERE CREATED BY DP AUTUMN DURALD ARKAPAW!

Before getting to work, a DP talks to the director and figures out what she wants the color palette and mood of the movie to be. She might do some research and print out a bunch of shots from different movies that have a similar look and feel to what the director wants, then look through them and get some inspiration. This process is how she pinpoints the right visual style for the film.

eeeeeee

Speaking of color palettes and mood, for *Sasha Versus Zombies* those are the first things the DP needs to figure out. If the movie is going to be scary, then maybe going for a darker color palette and lighting like *The Walking Dead* would be a good idea. Or perhaps the director wants the movie to be humorous, so the DP could look to a movie like *Halloweentown,* which is brighter and sillier. Or maybe the director wants a little bit of both, so the DP might look at something that is both creepy and colorful like *The Chilling Adventures of Sabrina.*

To help achieve the exact look and feel the director wants, the DP chooses specific types of camera lenses, filters, and lighting set-ups to change how the scene will appear in the film once it's captured. Once she and the director decide on what the movie is going to look like, then the DP makes a list of all the gear she needs, so the producer can rent it for her. She also starts making a list of the people she wants the producer to hire for her camera crew—this is another great example of how the producer's organizing skills are super important for making cool creative stuff happen.

The way filmmakers start to get their projects looking less like a pile of words and more like a movie is with *storyboards*. To do this, the director and the DP work with a *storyboard artist*, who is someone that draws simple sketches of the scenes in the screenplay, from the camera angles the director wants to use. She translates the screenplay into a more visual form. Storyboards don't need to be fancy or extra detailed, so a storyboard artist usually isn't a perfectionist about her work. For her, it is more important to translate a director's idea of a shot onto paper effectively.

With the help of the storyboards, the director can see where everything and everyone is going to be in each scene, and the DP can plan how the camera is going to move to capture what is happening. Working on storyboards together is a great opportunity for brainstorming and collaboration between the director and the DP. Because they have to decide how to shoot each scene, how everything will be arranged in the frame, how the scene will be lit, where the camera will be, and how it will move, the storyboards are a *really* helpful tool to make sure the director and the DP are both on the same page and know what to do. Using storyboards during pre-production to figure this out beforehand saves valuable time when the movie is being shot.

Let's think about how the opening scene of *Sasha Versus Zombies* would look as a bunch of storyboards.

INT. SASHA'S BEDROOM—AFTERNOON

Sasha sits at her makeup table, working on an extravagant eyeshadow look and dancing to pop music. Just as she starts singing into one of her makeup brushes—DING!

The doorbell rings and it surprises her.

SASHA
(yelling)
Coming!

She drops the brush and starts running through her house to the front door.

For example, if the director wants to shoot it as if the camera is the mirror, so Sasha is looking right at the audience, the storyboard for the shot would look like a simple sketch of a teenage girl, applying eyeshadow, singing, and looking right at the viewer. (That also means a really bright ring light will be on for Sasha's makeup, which is something the DP will have to consider when she's planning the lighting for this scene.)

For these storyboards, the storyboard artist would draw a big grid of boxes. In each box is a sketch of each little moment. Sasha putting on makeup. Sasha singing. Sasha looking surprised. This is how storyboard artists break down whole scenes into small parts.

Storyboards kind of look like panels in a comic book, but with no color and not a lot of detail. The storyboard artist's job is to capture the camera angle and *composition*, which is just how everything in the frame is arranged, of the shot. If you think being a storyboard artist is the job for you, then one thing you can do to practice your skills is to pay attention to the position of the camera and how a scene looks the next time you're watching a movie. Is the camera angle high or low? Is it close up or far away? Storyboard artists are good at drawing different perspectives and angles, as well as drawing people in a ton of different poses. It's pretty cool to think that a storyboard artist helps capture what each shot is supposed to show the audience and how it's supposed to make them feel.

llllllll

Alright, so at this point in pre-production, the DP and the storyboard artist are working on how the movie is going to be shot. At the same time, the director and producer need to start planning *what* is going to be shot. Preparing to shoot a movie is usually either about how to point the camera or what the camera is going to be pointing at. While the storyboard artist is going through the script and creating storyboards, the producer needs to find and hire another important member of the crew: the *production designer*.

A production designer is basically the queen of a movie's art department, and she plays a key role in making the film, so it's important that she is hired early during pre-production. The production designer is responsible for making sure that whatever is in front of the camera looks exactly right. This means coordinating all the visual elements—like the set and the costumes—so they all work together and are captured well on film.

The job of production designer involves a lot of imagination because she needs to fill in all the visual details of each scene. Things you might not think are all that important like furniture, or the wallpaper, or the flowers arranged on a doorstep were all considered and specifically placed by the production designer. All these details help tell the story, even if they seem like they don't matter that much.

The production designer imagines how someone's character is reflected in the space around them and how the themes of the movie are shown in the scene. For *Little Women*, Greta Gerwig wanted the audience to "feel the warmth of the March home in the middle of winter." You can see how the production designer made sure the inside of the home looked warm and cozy to match the director's vision. Production designers are always working on something different and challenging, depending on the film, from a cozy home in *Little Women* to a dazzling spaceship in *Jupiter Ascending*.

HANNAH BEACHLER WAS THE FIRST-EVER FEMALE PRODUCTION DESIGNER TO WORK ON A MARVEL FILM (BLACK PANTHER) AND THE FIRST EVER BLACK WOMAN TO WIN AN OSCAR FOR PRODUCTION DESIGN. SHE ALSO WORKS ON BEYONCÉ'S MUSIC VIDEOS!

Making sure that her imagination doesn't outpace the budget is another part of a production designer's job. Finding the perfect balance between the production designer's imagination, the tone of the film, and the budget means doing a lot of research.

~~ℓℓℓℓℓℓℓℓ~~

When researching for a movie like *Sasha Versus Zombies*, the production designer might watch old zombie movies and pay attention to the *sets*, which are the places where a movie is shot. She'd also look at different styles of houses, teen bedrooms, and high schools for references. Then, once her research is complete, she sketches out her idea of what the different sets should look like.

Because the director wants *Sasha Versus Zombies* to have a bright, colorful tone, the production designer makes sure that the director's color palette is reflected in the design of the whole production. For a scene where Sasha and her friends are barricading the front door to keep the zombies out, the production designer chooses pink see-through curtains for Sasha's living room, so the outlines of all the zombies outside can still be seen. Bright *and* creepy!

At the start of *Sasha Versus Zombies*, Sasha is in her bedroom, which is an easy set to find, design, and build. Next, the zombies come to Sasha's house, she puts zombie makeup on herself and her friends, and then the four of them escape through the backyard. During the middle of the film, the group makes their way through the suburban neighborhood, then to the high school where the final showdown takes place. So, those are the three main locations that the production designer must think about for the sets: Sasha's house, her suburban neighborhood, and her high school.

When it comes to sets and locations, the director and producer have a big decision to make. Where will they shoot the movie?

One option is to shoot the film in a movie *studio*. Many movie studios have huge indoor spaces that can be turned into anything from a haunted house to a jungle. The second option is to shoot it *on location*. This means that the film crew would need to find a real house, real neighborhood, and real high school to film in.

There are a lot of pros and cons to both choices. For example, it's usually more expensive to shoot in a studio, but you've got total control of the space so you can make it look however you want. If you shoot on location, pre-production will usually take less time, since instead of having to build an entire set, it's already made. It's much easier to prepare a bedroom that already exists instead of having to build one from scratch!

Regardless of where you shoot, the film crew will find a way to work their magic, so what would you like to do?

A. Shoot the movie at a location.

Continue to the next page.

B. Shoot the movie in a studio.

Flip to page 26.

RESIDENCE EVIL

SHOOTING ON LOCATION IS GREAT, BUT OF COURSE, FIRST YOU'VE got to find just the right spot.

There are a lot of factors to consider besides "does this place look cool?" You also have to consider, does the place have electricity? Room for a whole film crew to park? Is there anything noisy around, like an airport? When you watch a movie, it is easy to be awed by the amazing scenery, but shooting on location involves a ton of logistics.

It's a *location manager*'s job to find locations for movie shoots. Whether a movie needs a high school or a campground, a ballroom or an ice cream shop, she'll find the right place. To help with this task, location managers keep a big database of locations that can be used for filmmaking, including indoor places, outdoor places, historical places, new places, beautiful places, scary places, and any place in between. A location manager never knows what sort of place a producer will ask her to find, so it's always best to be prepared.

After she finds the right location for the film, she also needs to stay and work with the producer to manage it. She'll start by figuring out who she needs to talk with to rent the place, then she works with the producer to figure out how many days they need to rent the location for, how much it's going to cost, and what the rules of the location are. Maybe no dogs are allowed or maybe the film crew needs to leave by a certain time each day; maybe it's a fancy old mansion and the crew needs to be extra careful not to scratch the floor. Once the movie starts shooting, it is her job to make sure that the film crew follows these rules.

Location managers are experts at finding the perfect place to shoot a movie that looks great, works out logistically, *and* fits the budget of the project.

To check out a location, the producer will plan a walkthrough with the director, DP, and production designer so they can all inspect the place before they film in it. This is known as a *tech scout*, and it is done to find any problems or challenges the film crew might have with the location, like needing extra lighting in a particular area. You know, tech stuff. The tech scout might reveal that the location won't work, and the location manager will need to find a substitute.

Even with a great location, sometimes compromises have to be made. What if the high school meets all the logistical needs, but it's painted a weird color? What if it looks perfect, but the parking lot is tiny? What if it's an old, abandoned high school, and the electricity doesn't work anymore? That means it's time for some problem solving and a little movie magic.

Sasha Versus Zombies is set in Southern California, so the director wouldn't want Sasha's house to be an old-timey colonial house that looks like it belongs in New England. She'd feel the same way about the high school building. It would have to look like a real high school on the West Coast, not a huge brick building that is hundreds of years old.

While the location manager is searching for the right building to match the director's vision, she coordinates with the producer on scheduling. Because they're filming at a real high school, the producer needs to make sure the shoot happens during the summer, when there's no one around. Or that the shoot happens in an old high school building that isn't being used anymore. It would be tough to shoot a movie in between class periods!

Once the location manager finds the perfect match for all the locations in *Sasha Versus Zombies* and those locations pass a tech scout, the production designer begins her work of transforming them into Sasha's world.

A. Continue to the next page.

DAY
SIXTY

ZOMBIE HIGH SCHOOL

I N THE MOVIEMAKING WORLD, *SET* MEANS THE SCENERY ARRANGED for filming. It's basically just the setting that the camera is pointing at, whether it's a bedroom or a backyard.

For the sets, the production designer collaborates closely with someone known as the *art director*, who is her right-hand person. The art director oversees what's called the *art department*, the team responsible for the overall look of the sets for the movie. Altogether, the members of the art department design, decorate, and sometimes build all the sets.

Art directors are detail-oriented people. As well as all the creative stuff, art directors do a lot of administrative work, too. They'll work out a budget for all the materials needed, from wood to paint to nails; hire crew members; and keep track of the pre-production schedule: what needs to be made by what date. Art directors have an awesome combination of imagination and organization.

DOROTHEA HOLT REDMOND, WHO IS IN THE ART DIRECTORS GUILD HALL OF FAME, WORKED ON SEVERAL ALFRED HITCHCOCK FILMS AND HELPED DESIGN PORTIONS OF DISNEYLAND!

A key part of the art department is the *set decorator*, who is the woman responsible for getting background objects like furniture and decor situated how the art director wants them. The items she works with are called *set dressing*. Set dressing does not go on a salad. It's the objects in the background of a scene, from curtains to paintings to lamps. Adding these items to a set makes it feel more realistic, and it is up to the set decorator to work with her team, who are called *set dressers*, to get each set ready for the shoot.

Set dressing might be in the background, but it's still an important part of building a scene. It helps convey the story to the audience: genre, mood, time period, location, and even character can all be shown through the objects, decorations, and furniture in a scene. This is especially important with a historical movie. Imagine a flat-screen TV on the wall of a room set in the medieval times!

A viewer can sometimes tell what's going on with a character by what the space looks like around them. For example, a person sitting on the sofa in a dimly lit living room surrounded by empty ice cream cartons suggests to the viewer that the character is sad or lonely and maybe had a really bad day.

Along with character and mood, set dressing can also help convey the genre of the movie. You could very easily tell that you're watching a science fiction movie with one look at a laboratory set filled with futuristic gadgets.

That's what's fun about decorating a set—being able to tell so much story with just little details. For example, say there's a scene in a living room decorated with a big Christmas tree, lots of lights, piles of presents, and a roaring fire in the fireplace— what can you tell about what's going on? Well, it's got to be close to Christmas, so it's probably wintertime. With a fire roaring, that means it's cold. Lots of electric lights means it's modern day, not a movie set in another time period. The piles of presents are a hint that there is a big family living in the house. Just from all this set dressing, you have a lot of information about the scene.

Anyone working in the art department should be detail oriented and knowledgeable about design, lighting, and different paints and textiles. The art director and set decorator will have meetings to coordinate with the rest of the film crew and make sure that everything is coming together visually as planned and aligns with the director's vision for the movie.

Maybe the set decorator wants to use a detailed wallpaper for a certain set, but the DP wants to use very low lighting when the crew shoots there. In low light, the details in the wallpaper won't be seen. Knowing what sort of lighting the DP wants to use, the set decorator can choose a better wallpaper that will look great on camera.

If you're interested in the art department and love movies, there are many apprenticeships to apply to. The Art Directors Guild has programs to help budding artists learn about the industry. Many art directors and set dressers started their careers working on small, low-budget films with their friends, so keep an eye out in your community for any local filmmakers who might want some help!

ееееееее

For the big ending set in the high school, the *Sasha Versus Zombies* film crew needs to transform a regular high school location into a high school assaulted by the undead. While the building might still look normal on the outside, when you step inside, it's a totally different world.

To transform the interior of the high school into a zombie attack zone, the art department adds splashes of dried fake blood on the floor and across the lockers, pieces of foam painted to look like wood barricades leaning up against the windows, and chains hung across some of the doors to keep them shut against zombies.

The set decorator might have read the script and decided that the zombies would have tried to smash the windows of the high school, so she decorates them with decals to make it look like they've been broken. Plus, it looks a lot scarier because it seems like the zombies could come back and break in through the windows at any moment. Pretty cool, huh?

While the art department works on the high school set—as well as the house and neighborhood nearby—it's time to start finding the right person to transform into Sasha herself!

A. Flip to page 29.

DAY SIXTY

THE BUILD
WITCH PROJECT

▾▾▾●▾●▾▾▾●▾▾▾●▾▾▾●▾▾▾▾▾●▾●▾▾▾▾●▾▾▾●▾▾▾●

SHOOTING A MOVIE ON A *STUDIO LOT* SOUNDS FANCY, BUT A STUDIO lot is just a compound of office buildings and big indoor stages where movies and TV shows are made. The *back lot* on a studio lot is a place with buildings and outdoor spaces to shoot. In the moviemaking world, *set* means the scenery arranged for filming. It's basically just the setting that the camera is pointing at, whether it's a bedroom, an airplane, or a cave. Studio lots have sets made to look like city neighborhoods or houses that stay up all the time and just get redecorated for each movie.

While studio sets might look like real neighborhoods or houses when you see them on the screen, they usually are not fully functional. Only the parts that are seen on camera need to look real, so the art department doesn't have to build a full room or building with plumbing and electricity. Behind houses on a studio lot, there's usually just a blank wall!

> SCENES FILMED IN MOVIE STUDIOS ARE OFTEN SHOT IN FRONT OF GREEN SCREENS.
> GREEN SCREENS—GREEN BECAUSE IT IS THE MOST DIFFERENT FROM HUMAN
> SKIN COLORS!—ARE JUST THAT, GREEN BACKDROPS THAT A COMPUTER ARTIST
> CAN DIGITALLY REMOVE AND REPLACE WITH SOMETHING ELSE, SUCH AS A BUSTLING
> CITY BACKGROUND, STARRY NIGHT SKY, OR LUSH FOREST. USING THEM,
> A DIRECTOR CAN GET A DIGITAL SET EXTENSION AND HAVE A SCENE SHOT IN
> A STUDIO ROOM LOOK LIKE IT WAS SHOT OUTSIDE!

To create the sets, the production designer collaborates closely with someone known as the *art director*, who is her right-hand person. The art director oversees what's called the *art department*, the team responsible for the overall look of the sets for the movie. Altogether, the members of the art department design, decorate, and sometimes build all the sets.

Art directors are detail-oriented people. As well as all the creative stuff, art directors do a lot of administrative work, too. They'll work out a budget for all the materials needed, from wood to paint to nails; hire crew members; and keep track of the pre-production schedule: what needs to be made by what date. Art directors have an awesome combination of imagination and organization.

The women in charge of building the sets with their bare hands and making them look good are the *set builders* and *set painters*. Like their name says, set builders are the women who create sets out of wood, metal, or whatever materials are needed to make the set look realistic, without being too expensive or fragile. In fact, tons of movie sets are built out of materials like plywood and even cardboard, which helps save the production crew a ton of money.

Once the builders are finished, set painters paint backdrops or any other part of the set. With the right combination of construction and paint, a big piece of cardboard can transform into the rusty interior of a submarine or the parlor walls of a beautiful, historic mansion. If you are looking for a job that allows you to work with your hands and be creative, then these are two roles on a film crew for you.

It is a lot of work, but building and painting a set allows total creative control. With the set made from scratch, the art department can choose everything from the paint colors on the wall to the type of flooring, and more. Most sets are built from sheets of plywood mounted on a giant wood frame called *flats*. These are then screwed together to form fake rooms or other spaces. Once the room is constructed, all sorts of finishes can go on them, from fancy wallpaper to a lining that looks like concrete. Making sets is pretty cool and a lot of work, but it never gets boring!

If you're interested in the art department and love movies, there are many apprenticeships to apply to. The Art Directors Guild has programs to help budding artists learn about the industry. Many art directors and set dressers started their careers working on small, low-budget films with their friends, so keep an eye out in your community for any local filmmakers who might want some help!

ееееееее

To shoot *Sasha Versus Zombies* in a studio, the production designer and art director build a set to look like Sasha's bedroom. To do so, they transform an empty warehouse inside one of the studio buildings. When they're finished, the only thing that looks different from a real bedroom is that one of the walls is missing. They don't need to build all the walls to make it look like a real bedroom on camera, and also, having one side be totally open will be helpful when they're filming. They wouldn't have to worry about fitting all the camera equipment into a small bedroom. If you weren't looking at it through a camera lens, Sasha's bedroom sort of looks like a gigantic dollhouse.

After the sets are all built and painted, the production designer and art director come in and create the perfect bedroom for a teenage makeup fanatic. It has bright

curtains and bright bedclothes, with posters of her favorite cosplayers and makeup artists plastered all over the walls. Sasha's vanity table needs to be a makeup artist's dream, with a huge light-up mirror.

While the art department is transforming the sets into Sasha's home, it's time to find an actress to transform into Sasha!

A. Continue to the next page.

CAST OF THE DEAD

A T THIS STAGE IN PRE-PRODUCTION, BEFORE ANY MORE CREW CAN be hired, a movie needs to be *cast*. The cast of a movie is the group of actors playing all the different roles, from the main characters, or *leads*, to smaller, or *supporting*, roles, to roles that might only have a little bit of dialogue, or *lines*.

Some directors might already have an idea of who they want to play the characters or ideas about what they are supposed to look like, or they might want to have *auditions* so different actors can try out for the role to see whether they're a good fit. Regardless of how the actors are chosen in the end, the person who finds all these actors is the *casting director*.

A good casting director has an eye for acting talent and a fabulous memory. Casting directors meet a ton of people and see a ton of performances, so it really helps to be able to remember names and faces as much as possible. That way, when a director asks for a group of cool teens to fight some zombies, she'll be able to think of the perfect actors that fit the role. It's a lot of fun to find the right actor for the right movie!

Usually (unless the actor is already very famous), the casting process begins with a casting director showing the producer and director a bunch of *headshots*—glossy, professional photos of actors. She'll pick a bunch for each role. Sometimes, she'll send the actors a scene from the script and have them record an *audition tape* for the director to watch.

For each movie, the casting process is always a little different. A director may know exactly who she wants to play the lead roles. Or she may want to see a bunch of different audition tapes and meet with a bunch of different actors. She may even think she knows exactly who she wants to play the role, then sees someone completely different who is an even better fit.

AULI'I CRAVALHO WAS A LAST-MINUTE ADDITION TO THE LIST OF GIRLS AUDITIONING FOR THE VOICE ROLE OF MOANA, BUT SHE ENDED UP BEING THE PERFECT PERSON FOR THE ROLE!

Once a director decides on the actors she wants, the casting director is responsible for making sure that the actors will be available when the movie is being filmed and that the producer can afford to hire them. Usually, the more famous an actor is, the more money a production will have to pay them.

Throughout the shooting of the movie, the casting director also handles all the cast-related problems and takes care of everything the actors need. If someone is going to be late, if someone has dietary restrictions, if someone isn't happy with their costume, then she is on it.

eeeeeeee

To start, the casting director would read the script and figure out all the people who need to be cast for the whole film. She needs four teenagers to play Sasha and her three friends, so one lead and three supporting roles. Not only does the casting director find potential actors for each role; she also works with the director and producer to decide which one is the best fit for the role.

Many factors go into the decision to cast an actor. While the actor should match the look that the director wants and be talented at acting, there's a lot more to it than that. Each actor brings something unique—their own personal interpretation—to the role.

Five different actresses might play Sasha in five completely different ways. One actress might read Sasha's lines with a lot of humor and sarcasm, while another actress might be more serious. One actress might play Sasha as very nervous and scared, while another actress might play Sasha as fearless and full of fire. That's the magic of working with actors! It's also why casting directors come up with several options for each role.

LEGENDARY CASTING DIRECTOR MARION DOUGHERTY, WHO CAST MOVIES LIKE GREASE, BRAVEHEART, AND BATMAN, SAID, "NO CASTING DIRECTOR CAN TRULY SAY, 'I KNEW HE [OR SHE] WAS GONNA BE A STAR' BECAUSE THAT'S A BUNCH OF BALONEY. CASTING IS A GAME OF GUT INSTINCT. YOU FEEL THEIR TALENT AND POTENTIAL IN THE PIT OF YOUR STOMACH. IT'S ABOUT GUTS AND LUCK."

So, the casting director finds and works with all the lead actors and the other actors with speaking parts, but what about everyone else? Who finds all the actors to fill the nonspeaking, or *background*, roles?

The question the team needs to answer now is whether or not to hire people for a bunch of background roles in *Sasha Versus Zombies*. Going through the script, there are definitely scenes where having many people in the background would be a great addition, such as groups of other zombie-attack survivors at the high school at the end. Of course, this decision depends on a few factors.

The upside to having background actors is that they can make a scene feel more like real life, and certainly more cinematic. However, they cost money. Not only do you have to hire the actors; you have to budget for the extra costumes, hair and makeup, and all that. It can add a lot to the look of a movie, but it can also add a lot to the budget. Without background actors, the production crew will save money, but the movie will be more focused on Sasha and her friends.

For *Sasha Versus Zombies*, what do you think would be the best way to go?

A. You decide to hire background actors.

   Flip to the next page.

B. You decide to save money and not use any background actors.

   Flip to page 33.

US

D IRECTORS CAN'T JUST GRAB A BUNCH OF RANDOM FOLKS TO BE IN the background of a scene. It's harder than people realize! Acting as if you are on a date in a bar, or on the phone in an office, or walking your dog takes acting skill. *Background actors* are all the people in these roles who help fill in the backgrounds of the scenes. This means all the folks you see in a movie who are walking down the street, sitting in a restaurant, or dancing in a nightclub. They used to be called "extras," but they definitely aren't extra. These actors can be crucial in making a scene look realistic.

So, you decided to hire background actors, but who is going to wrangle them all?

A *background casting director* handles everything related to background actors. She finds them, hires them, and manages them. Whether it's a bunch of customers in a coffee shop, families vacationing on a beach, or just random people walking around a neighborhood, the background casting director casts them all. Like a casting director, she has a big database of actors of all ages and genders ready and available to call for jobs.

A background casting director works with actors who are both talented and reliable. She'll work with the director to find all the people needed for each scene and make sure they show up on time, wearing what they are supposed to be wearing.

For a teen zombie movie, the background casting director needs a bunch of teenagers, a bunch of zombies, and then some people to fill out the neighborhood. Lawn-mowing dads, dog walkers, and other residents. Maybe even some freaked-out parents and teachers who can show up at the high school with the other survivors.

Just like the casting director, the background casting director uses the script breakdown to plan out how many actors she needs to find and hire. She'll go through each scene to figure out the background actor requirements. She's got to be extremely organized—it would be bad to send all the lawn-mowing dads on the day a bunch of teenagers are needed!

Now that the casting and background casting directors have found some great actors, it's time to start thinking about what they're all going to wear!

A. Continue to the next page.

KILLER COSTUMES
FROM OUTER SPACE

JUST LIKE REAL-LIFE PEOPLE WHO ARE GETTING READY TO GO TO school or work, outfits are important to movie characters, no matter what genre they're in.

Costumes are essential both for the production design and for character development in a film. They contribute to the look of a movie, and they help the actors wearing them really get into playing their character. Even if it's just a T-shirt and jeans, the best costumes are well thought out, and great *costume designers* consider both how a costume will show a character's personality as well as how it works with the other visuals in a scene. Sometimes, they are really complex, like Ruth E. Carter's Oscar-winning costume designs for *Black Panther*, or they're normal clothes like Amy Parris's costumes for *Stranger Things*. There are so many iconic costumes, from Trinity's all-black pleather in *The Matrix* to the whole cast's outfits in *The Breakfast Club*. Can you imagine Dorothy without her ruby red slippers?

Since it's important that the costumes work with the rest of the production design and with the way the director wants the characters to look, costume designers consult the producer, director, and production designer on how the costumes will look. Then, after talking with the team, the costume designer begins her research and starts sketching out ideas, just like a production designer does. She'll also look through the script breakdown to figure out what kinds of costumes are needed—and how many. When the designs are finished, she'll either rent the outfits she needs or hire a team to help make the costumes before scheduling fittings for the actors.

A costume designer should be knowledgeable about many different aspects of clothes and fashion. It comes in handy for her to know fashion history, in case she works on a historical, or *period*, movie. Artistic knowledge is also very helpful because the costumes for a film often must work with a specific color palette that the director has chosen. Alexandra Byrne, who was the costume designer for *Emma*, created designs that worked within director Autumn de Wilde's color palette of soft pastels. Finally, a costume designer should be skilled at sewing and constructing clothes, especially if she's working on a fantasy or science fiction film that calls for clothes that can't be easily picked up at a store, such as Ngila Dickson's Oscar-award-winning costume designs for *The Lord of the Rings*. It's tough to find an elf costume at the mall!

There is never just one version of a character's costume. A costume designer will read through the script and keep track of all the changes a costume needs to go through. Sasha's outfit will become progressively bloodier and more torn up as she fights more and more zombies throughout the film. What that means is the costume designer will have to have several versions of Sasha's costume, all in various stages of goriness.

It wouldn't do to have Sasha at the end of a big zombie fight wearing a sparkling clean shirt! So, a costume designer's job includes designing and making the costumes but also planning for how those costumes are going to change throughout the film. If she ends up buying the clothes or renting the clothes for the movie, instead of making them herself, she'll buy a bunch of them, in different sizes too, just in case.

Just like in everyday life, what we wear shows off a lot of our personality or sometimes how we're feeling that day. Figuring out how to highlight certain parts of Sasha's personality is all part of a day's work for the costume designer for *Sasha Versus Zombies*. Obviously, picking out clothes and outfits is super fun, but it's also so interesting to tell a story with costumes and to change a character's outfits to reflect how they grow and experience the events of the movie.

While the costume designer is working on the costumes, a *film hairstylist* works on the hairstyles. The hairstylist is the woman responsible for both designing all the hairstyles for a film's characters as well as styling it on set while the movie is shooting. The *makeup artist* creates the makeup designs for all the characters and applies them to the actors during the shoot. Both women work closely together and with the costume designer to create the overall look for each character.

Some of the most memorable, and enviable, looks in film history, from Princess Leia's space buns in *Star Wars* to Nancy's eyeliner in *The Craft*, were created by makeup and hair artists. Just like their outfits, hair styles and makeup can be a crucial part of crafting a character.

Film hairstylists sometimes work with an actor's existing hair, either by cutting or dyeing it in addition to styling it, but they also work with bald caps and wigs. Since it is really important to make sure that none of the products and procedures damage an actor's skin or hair, many hairstylists and makeup artists start their careers by getting their cosmetology license before moving on to work in film.

Okay, this is for all the human, non-zombie characters.

What about the *zombies*?

Well, that's a big question for any film production. First, the team has to decide whether the zombies, creatures, monsters, and so on are going to be *practical effects*, made with costuming and makeup, or made from *CGI*, computer generated imagery. Of course, there are pros and cons to both. It is sometimes much easier for a team to do more jaw-dropping, over-the-top stuff with CGI—imagine gigantic dragons breathing fire, hordes of goblins, wands shooting magic spells. However, choosing CGI effects means *a lot* more time needed to digitally create them after the shoot ends. Making the zombies with practical effects means it will take more time during the shoot, but it often looks more real, and it's easier for the actors to do their job when they aren't working with a green screen.

A. You choose to create zombies with practical effects.

Flip to the next page.

B. You choose to create zombies with CGI.

Flip to page 39.

SOMETHING LATEX THIS WAY COMES

ZOMBIES, VAMPIRES, WEREWOLVES, FAIRIES, EVIL SKELETONS, aliens, and even the pointy ears of elves. All these fantastical creatures can be made by a *special effects makeup artist*, or *SFX makeup artist*.

She is responsible for creating special makeup effects and anything that is beyond more traditional beauty makeup. Black eyes, monster makeup, prosthetic noses, goblin ears, bloody wounds—she can do it all!

A SFX makeup artist usually attends school to get special training in advanced makeup techniques and to learn how to use all the materials required for effects; however, there is a growing community of self-taught artists as well. Liquid latex, foam latex, and paint are only some of the materials they use regularly. While it seems like a no-brainer that these artists are in demand for movies that feature zombies, monsters, and other supernatural creatures, SFX artists are also needed for effects that might seem a little more . . . normal. They also know how to do things like add bald caps and wrinkles to make an actor look much older or use makeup, paint, and prosthetics to add bruises and cuts to an actor for her fight scene.

Prosthetics are an important and very cool part of an SFX artist's job. They are tricky to use, require a lot of patience and know-how to apply correctly, and come in almost any size and shape you can think of. To make prosthetics that fit perfectly onto a specific actor, many SFX artists will make a mold of the actor's face—or sometimes their whole body!—and then sculpt the prosthetics, using clay, right onto it. It's helpful to keep this mold, in case the SFX artist needs to make more prosthetics. In fact, in *The Lord of the Rings*, Liv Tyler's elf ears were made out of gelatin, like Jell-O, and melted in the rain, so they had to make hundreds of versions of them!

MANY OF THE MOST FAMOUS SFX MAKEUP DESIGNS HAVE BEEN CREATED BY WOMEN. VE NEILL, WHO RUNS HER OWN SFX SCHOOL IN LOS ANGELES, HAS BEEN NOMINATED FOR EIGHT OSCARS FOR HER WORK ON SUCH MOVIES AS BEETLEJUICE, PIRATES OF THE CARIBBEAN, EDWARD SCISSORHANDS, AND MRS. DOUBTFIRE. ONE OF THE MOST FAMOUS CLASSIC HORROR MONSTERS OF ALL TIME, THE CREATURE FROM CREATURE FROM THE BLACK LAGOON, WAS DESIGNED BY A WOMAN, MILICENT PATRICK.

For the zombies in *Sasha Versus Zombies*, the SFX artist gets started by finding out how many zombies she will have to create before she gets to designing and molding the pieces that will be added onto the zombie actors.

THERE ARE ACTORS WHO ARE SPECIALLY TRAINED TO PLAY CREATURES AND ZOMBIES. MORGANA IGNIS WORE ALL SORTS OF PROSTHETICS AND COSTUMES FOR THE HORROR SHOW STAN AGAINST EVIL, WHERE SHE PLAYED A HOST OF MONSTERS, INCLUDING A WITCH, A DEMON, AND A VAMPIRE.

Depending on the director's vision, she might make all sorts of makeup designs with rotting lips, bulging eyeballs, broken jaws, bloody limbs—you know, the works. She also needs to think about how many zombies will be in a scene and how long they will be there. The more screen time a zombie gets, the more thought she'll want to put into its look. Once she goes through the script breakdown to figure out how many zombies she needs and how complicated their makeups are going to be, the SFX artist will start ordering supplies and hiring a team to help her. Then, she'll meet with the producer and work out how much prep time will be needed every day the zombies are on set. SFX makeup can take a lot of time—sometimes up to eight hours!—so it's important that the producers factor that into their schedules. The makeups also take time to remove, so the team has to make sure to schedule time for that, as well. Can't let anyone go home still covered in fake blood!

While the SFX makeup artist handles all the special effects that go on actors, for things like weapons and tools to fight the zombies, you've got to head to the prop shop.

A. Continue to the next page.

DAY ONE HUNDRED AND FIVE

PROP MASTERS
OF THE UNIVERSE

PROPS ARE SHORT FOR *PROPERTY*, AND THEY'RE BASICALLY ANY object in a movie that is used by the actors. Props include everything from weapons to hairbrushes. Someone has got to be in charge of all the stuff in a movie, and the woman responsible for finding, making, renting, storing, transporting, and managing all the props is known as the *prop master*.

> THE DIFFERENCE BETWEEN A PROP AND SET DRESSING IS THAT A PROP IS AN OBJECT THAT IS HANDLED BY THE ACTOR, WHILE SET DRESSING IS AN OBJECT IN THE BACKGROUND OF A SCENE. A MIRROR HANGING ON A WALL IN A ROOM IS SET DRESSING, WHILE A HAND MIRROR THAT THE ACTOR USES DURING THE SCENE IS A PROP.

Just like many of the other team members, the prop master works off the script breakdown. First, she goes through and figures out all the various props that are needed for each scene. If it's a more fantastical film or a genre film, she will often have to make the props, which could be anything from alien laser guns to a witch's spell book and other items she won't be able to easily find and buy online or at a store.

> PROP MASTER TRISH GALLAHER GLENN WORKED ON DISNEY'S RECENT REBOOT OF THE MUPPETS AND HAD TO MAKE MUPPET-SIZED PROPS, INCLUDING ROLLING PINS FOR THE SWEDISH CHEF AND INSTRUMENTS FOR THE BAND. SHE MADE MORE THAN ONE THOUSAND PROPS FOR THE MOVIE!

Even if a film is not fantastical, sometimes special props need to be made to keep everyone safe. Since actors rarely handle real weapons, a prop master might make weapons out of rubber or foam so that no one gets hurt—also because they are much easier to carry. *Hero weapons* and *props* are the weapons or props the prop master makes with real metal and wood, with all the correct details, to be used for closeups.

Craftsmanship is the name of the game for prop masters, and it's important for them to know how to work with all sorts of different building materials. Every movie is different and presents unique challenges. Often, she will have a team of people who help make the props, called *prop fabricators.*

Another skill a prop master should have, besides making the stuff, is keeping it all organized. Many prop masters save their props because you never know when something will come in handy for another movie. It's a huge waste of time and money if she can't find what she needs quickly! Whether it's feather quills, plastic skulls, footballs, wands, or Slinkies, everything needs to have its place. Like the costume designer, sometimes the prop master will make something, but other times, it is much easier if she just buys it.

The prop master is responsible for hiring her team of fabricators as well as for creating a schedule of when the props are brought to the set and when they need to be returned to the warehouse. Often, a film team will hire people known as *production buyers* who do all the shopping for the production designer, the costume designer, and the prop master, so that they can all focus on designing and not waste time running around to different stores.

When you watch a movie, pay attention to the props being used by the actors. See what you notice, whether any props tell you more about the character using them or are important to the story.

≈≈≈≈≈≈≈

The prop master needs to make different versions of the weapons Sasha and her friends use to fight off the undead. As the group makes their way through the neighborhood, Sasha uses a baseball bat to pummel some zombies. One version is the bat when she first finds it in her backyard, while it's clean and not covered in zombie gore. Another is the bat totally covered in dark fake blood after Sasha gets in some zombie battles. Although they look like regular wooden bats, both versions are made from foam. Movie magic!

The prop master goes through the script and works with the production designer on what props she needs to make or rent for each scene: household items like pillows and makeup brushes for Sasha's room, weapons for the flight through the neighborhood, and maybe errant school supplies being used as barricades against the zombies when Sasha and her friends finally make it to the high school.

Even if a movie is shot on location, the filmmakers will still need props. It wouldn't do for Sasha to have an empty bedroom! Sometimes, props are essential to the story and are heavily featured on screen, like the baseball bat Sasha ends up fighting zombies with, or Rey's lightsaber, or Wonder Woman's sword. Other times, props might not be as noticeable, but they still add texture and a sense of authenticity to the scene, like Sasha's makeup mirror and the makeup kit in her room.

A. Continue to the next page.

RETURN OF
THE KILLER SPREADSHEETS

BEFORE PRE-PRODUCTION IS OVER AND THE NEXT STAGE OF FILM-making begins, the producer must hire one more important member of the film crew (and one of the most helpful for her).

While the producer watches over and is responsible for the whole project, a *line producer* is in charge of all the tiny details, like equipment rentals and the daily budget. A line producer is super organized and fantastic at keeping track of a million things. She is the queen of spreadsheets and lists, and she is always in the thick of it and part of all the action (while filling out a whole bunch of paperwork). In fact, many of the logistical issues of a film shoot are solved by a line producer so that the producer can focus on the bigger picture. Once everything is approved by the producer, the line producer will handle getting the DP her cameras, will work with the casting director to make sure the cast arrives at the set, and will make sure the production designer has all the materials she needs.

Even though she handles a lot of the smaller and more specific aspects of the shoot, her role is pivotal because many of the crew members answer to her. The line producer ends up being the producer's main connection to the rest of the film crew. Many line producers move on to become fully fledged producers.

The line producer will be a crucial presence on set when the movie starts filming. With her hired, it's time to start shooting!

A. **Flip to the next page.**

PRODUCTION

Now you are ready to start the production stage of filmmaking—you can call this stage *principal photography* if you're fancy. This is generally what everyone thinks of when they hear the words "making a movie"—it's the stage when the movie is actually filmed. All the writing, planning, designing, organizing, and preparation has been leading up to this moment.

Compared to the months—or sometimes years!—that a film can spend in development and pre-production, the production stage is relatively short. Unless it's a big, epic film, most movies take anywhere from a few weeks to a couple of months to shoot. But there's a *lot* to do in that short time. *Sasha Versus Zombies* still has to hire many more crew members, and many more decisions need to be made.

Flip to the next page to start filming the movie!

SHOOT OF THE LIVING DEAD

TO GET A MOVIE THROUGH THE DEVELOPMENT STAGE, THE FILM-making team uses the screenplay as a guide. In pre-production, it is the script breakdown that serves as the blueprint for the whole crew to prepare for shooting. A director's *shot list* is the north star for the production stage. A shot list is a document detailing all the shots needed for each scene—it's sort of a checklist. The goal of production is to get each shot checked off that list.

During production, there are what seem like a zillion things to do to get the movie made that don't even include shooting the actual movie. One of the first orders of business is to set up the production office.

This is the place where all the administrative stuff for managing an ongoing film production happens. It will open right before the shoot begins and stay open until it's over. Production offices are magical places that pop up, become a hub of frantic action while a movie is being shot, and then, *poof!* they disappear once production is done.

The woman managing the production office is called the *production coordinator*, and she is a crucial part of running the movie shoot smoothly. During the entirety of the shoot, the production coordinator works from the production office, which becomes her personal war room.

Right before production starts, she sets up the production office, gets all equipment (like computers and printers) organized, and orders a whole bunch of office supplies—highlighters, notebooks, paper clips, Post-its, tape, etc. This stuff isn't just useful for being in school; you need it to make a movie, too!

You know that saying, "An army marches on its stomach"? Well, a shoot marches on its paperwork. With so much equipment that needs to be rented, people who need to be at the right place at the right time, and documents that need to be printed out, the production office is like a massive steam engine fueled by paperwork.

When the shoot begins, the production coordinator is responsible for printing out and distributing any necessary paperwork and keeping track of all the crew members. Nothing happens on a film set without the production coordinator knowing about it. If any members of the cast or crew are flying in for the shoot, the production coordinator handles all their travel plans. She also makes sure that the cast all have copies of the script and shooting schedule.

There's another important part of a production coordinator's job—keeping the script up to date. Often, a script will undergo changes from the screenwriter or director right up until and sometimes even during the shoot. The director might have a meeting with one of the actors to change their lines, or the screenwriter might make a last-minute change to the ending. Either way, it's the production coordinator's responsibility to make sure that everyone in the cast and crew has the latest version of the script. The printer really gets a workout!

Being a production coordinator is certainly exciting, but it's also a lot of work. Luckily, she doesn't have to do it alone: she has a *production assistant* to help her.

A production assistant, or PA, does basically *everything*. She prints out scripts, runs errands, makes coffee, answers the phone, fixes emergencies, you name it, she does it. A movie couldn't function without the hard work of PAs.

If you want to get into the movie business, then this is the best place to start. No matter whether you want to be a producer or a prop master, a production assistant is the most common entry-level job in film (a.k.a. the easiest job to get). Working as a PA is a fantastic way to get practical knowledge about making movies and how different aspects and departments of a film set work. In fact, while some production assistants help out in the production office, others end up working all over the place, even on set during the shoot. Being a PA means getting to do a million different tasks and it is a lot of hectic work, but if you love movies, it can also be a really fun job!

> MANY WOMEN WHO START OUT AS PRODUCTION ASSISTANTS GO ON TO BECOME PRODUCTION COORDINATORS, PRODUCERS, OR DIRECTORS. EVEN SOME FAMOUS ACTRESSES, LIKE OCTAVIA SPENCER, STARTED OUT AS PRODUCTION ASSISTANTS!

Production assistants need to have top-notch teamwork and listening skills. Understanding her tasks, responsibilities, and timelines is crucial for the work of a PA, as is being efficient. Working as a PA is also a great way to meet other people who work in the movie business, so doing this job well could open the door to more opportunities to work on more movies!

Another important person in the production office is the *production accountant*. She's in charge of making sure the budget—or the movie itself—doesn't go off the rails.

Just like a regular accountant, she makes sure that a film isn't spending too much money, or *going over budget*. If a film production spends too much money too early during the making of the film, the rest of the production won't have any to use. Then if the movie runs out of money, the producers will have to find more investors or even shut down the shoot. Not good!

A production accountant keeps track of all the money a production is spending and what it is spent on—everything from cameras to pencils. She also keeps track of how much everyone is getting paid and makes sure they get their checks on time.

The production coordinator, accountant, and PAs form a sort of superhero team to keep the movie running smoothly. They do the paperwork, so the rest of the team can focus on their creativity.

Of all the paperwork printed out in the production office every day, the most crucial is the *call sheet*.

A call sheet lists all the key information about the day's shoot, from where everyone needs to be and what time they need to be there, to how long they need to be there and which scenes are going to be shot. The call sheet also lists *who* and *what* needs to be there. All the cast who will be in the scenes shot that day, all the crew members who need to be there, all the stuff that's required, including the costumes and props. The call sheet will also say where everyone needs to park, what the weather is going to be like, when everyone is going to have lunch, and tons of other important details like that. Without the almighty call sheet, the shoot would quickly fall apart.

The woman who makes the call sheet every day is the director's right-hand woman for the shoot, the *assistant director*. Also known as the AD, she runs the set during a movie shoot. She's the director's

CALL SHEET		FRI OCT 13
PRODUCTION COMPANY: BLACK LODGE PICTURES	**SASHA VS THE ZOMBIES**	**DAY 5 OF 25**
	SCRIPT VERSION: YELLOW	GENERAL CREW CALL 6:00AM / SHOOTING CALL 7:30AM / LUNCH 11:00AM
EXEC. PRODUCER: / PRODUCER: / LINE PRODUCER: / DIRECTOR/WRITER: / 1ST ASSISTANT DIRECTOR:	GENERAL CREW CALL 6:00AM	WEATHER / HIGH 55 SUNNY LOW 45 / SUNRISE 6:55

BASECAMP	PARKING	LOCATION(S)
PALMS PALMS PALMS HOTEL 112 AQUA PARKWAY HOLLYWOOD, CA	24H PARKING 35 EL CERRITOS	HOT BEAN SQUEEZINS 30 EL CERRITOS HOLLYWOOD, CA

SETS AND SCENE DESCRIPTION	SCENE	CAST	PAGES	LOCATION(S)
EXT. COFFEE SHOP ROOF — SASHA BEGINNING DESCENT ON LADDER	13	1	20	HOT BEAN SQUEEZINS
EXT. COFFEE SHOP ROOF — SASHA AND XICHELLE CALLING OVER RADIO	13	1,2	18	
INT. COFFEE SHOP — ZOMBIE EMERGING FROM ROASTED BEANS	10	3	13A	30 EL CERRITOS HOLLYWOOD, CA
INT. COFFEE SHOP — ZOMBIE FACING OF WITH SASHA	10	1,3	12	
INT. COFFEE SHOP — ZOMBIE FACING OF WITH SASHA	10	1,2,3	13B	
INT. COFFEE SHOP — ZOMBIE CHASING SASHA AND XICHELLE	10	1,2,3		

#	CAST	CHARACTER	CALL	SET	P/U	REPORT TO
1	SASHA	SASHA	7:30AM	9:00AM	N/A	HAIR/MAKEUP
2	MARISOL	XICHELLE	7:30AM	9:00AM	N/A	HAIR/MAKEUP
3	GUILLERMO	BARISTA ZOMBIE	11:30AM	1:30PM	N/A	HAIR/MAKEUP

EXTRAS, BACKGROUND				SPECIAL EQUIPMENT/MISC	
QTY	TYPE	CALL	SCENES	PROPS	SASHA'S BLOOD BAT
1	WEAP	8:30AM	10,13	SET DRESSING	
2	VIS	1:00PM	10	SPECIAL EFFECTS	SOFT-JELLY ZOMBIE HEAD

connection to the rest of the crew and keeps everyone in line and everything running according to plan. While the production coordinator makes sure everything is on schedule and going smoothly in the production office, the assistant director does the same thing but on set. She keeps track of the director's shot list so that each scene and shot on the schedule for that day is completed. Using the shot list, the AD checks the daily progress of the movie shoot against the overall shooting schedule to make sure the production isn't falling behind.

At the end of each day's shoot, the assistant director is the one who either hands out or emails the next day's call sheet. The PA prints them out at the production office and then drives the sheets over to the set.

Things can change at the last minute, so it's important that the AD stays on top of everything and makes sure the most up-to-the-second information is on the call sheet so that everyone can plan for the next day.

> PRODUCTION ASSISTANTS OFTEN GO ON TO BECOME ASSISTANT DIRECTORS, WHICH IS ANOTHER GREAT JOB FOR ANYONE LOOKING TO BECOME A DIRECTOR ONE DAY AND MAKE THEIR OWN MOVIES.

Along with keeping everything running smoothly on set, the assistant director also ensures that everything the director wants done is done, when she wants it done. This is another very hectic job, but if you want to be on a movie set all the time, it's the job for you. Being an AD involves getting up early in the morning and being good at giving clear directions to a lot of people. ADs are also first-class cat wranglers and make sure everyone who needs to be on set is present when they need to be there and that shooting starts on time.

Since she has a lot on her plate, sometimes the AD will get an assistant to help her. The main AD is called the *first* assistant director, and her assistant is called the *second* assistant director. Then, if a movie is *really* big, even the second assistant director will get an assistant, and she is called the *second second* assistant director, or "second-second" for short. Maybe it is because second-second is fun to say.

Okay, now that the production office is all set up and you've got your call sheet, you're ready to get to set. But, how do you get there?

In case you haven't noticed yet, when making a movie, every little detail needs to be figured out ahead of time, including transportation. Someone has to pick all the actors up from the hotel where they're staying, drive the big vans and trucks full of equipment, and find a place to park all the trailers. You might say that transportation needs to be . . . coordinated. Of course, that means there is a *transportation coordinator*. (Yes, there's a lot of types of coordinators on a movie crew.)

Transportation is an essential wheel in the logistical machine of moviemaking. A transportation, or just "transpo" for short, coordinator oversees all the transportation requirements for a film, whether that's moving people or equipment. Big rig trucks, trailers, limos, vans, buses, minibuses—you name it, she handles it.

Sometimes, on a really big budget movie, the transpo coordinator will hire a *transport captain* to help her. The transport captain focuses on handling the travel for the cast and the crew, so the transpo coordinator can focus on getting the equipment and trailers to the set. There usually is a team of multiple *drivers* who work for the transpo coordinator and are great at handling all kinds of different vehicles. They're definitely champions at parking.

A great transpo coordinator is punctual and pays close attention to detail. In addition to getting everyone where they need to go on time, she needs to make sure that all her vehicles are in tip-top shape and are safe to drive—and that the gas tanks are never empty! If the film shoot is on location out in the wilderness, for example, the transpo coordinator needs to make sure all her trucks and vans and cars can safely handle the rough roads.

Are you ready to head to the set?

A. Did you choose to shoot on location?

Continue to the next page.

B. Did you choose to shoot in a studio?

Flip to page 53.

THE CALIFORNIA LAWNMOWER MASSACRE

ON A FILM SET, EVERY DETAIL IS IMPORTANT . . . EVEN THE LAWN. While it might seem trivial, there is a lot that nature and plants can tell the audience about a scene. For example, in a movie, if the lawn of a house is all dried up and dead, then maybe the characters who live inside are too busy or sad to take care of it. If the lawn is perfectly green and cared for—too perfectly green and cared for—maybe the characters inside are very strict.

However the director wants the greenery to look, the *greensperson* is the woman who handles it. That's right, you can work with plants in the movie business! Greenspeople, sometimes known as greenskeepers, are sort of like the art department for plants. They take care of all grass, flowers, hedges, and any sort of landscaping material that's seen on screen. They've got to take care of everything green, even if it's plastic. This also means they keep an eye on non-plant stuff too, like the rocks around a garden, the sand on a beach, or even a pile of dirt.

Greenspeople are very creative and good at taking care of and growing plants, which means that they usually have an extensive knowledge of different kinds of plants. Depending on the movie, the greensperson might need to create the greenery from scratch, so it's important for her to have a working knowledge of the kinds of plants that grow in different areas and environments.

For a movie like *Sasha Versus Zombies* that takes place entirely in a suburb, the greensperson has to think about flora like lawns, flower beds, and shrubs. Since it's in Southern California, she might add palm trees, succulents, and other region-specific plants. She does her own script breakdown, looking through each scene to figure out what she needs for it. In front of Sasha's house, the greensperson and her team work with the production designer and art department to create a big, green lawn and trimmed hedges next to the front windows.

The greensperson must also plan for how the greenery will change in each scene. When the zombies try to break into Sasha's house, they're certainly not going to mind the hedges. Creating a stomped-on-by-zombies look for the front of the house will be just as important as creating the pristine-suburban-neighborhood look before they arrive.

With the exterior of the location handled, it's time for you to go inside to see where the camera department is setting up the first shot.

A. Continue to the next page.

HOCUS FOCUS

NOW THAT ALL THE ELEMENTS THAT GO IN FRONT OF THE CAMERA are ready—actors, sets, costumes, props—it's time to put together the lights and camera part of "Lights, camera, action!"

Before the cameras can start shooting, the scene needs to be lit. Literally. Remember how the director of photography—the DP—helps create the look of the movie by choosing lighting, lenses, and camera movement? Well, for the lighting aspect, the DP works with the *gaffer*. She is the one in control of all the lighting on the set. The DP will tell the gaffer what sort of lighting she wants, and then the gaffer works with her crew to make it happen.

She'll let the DP know what kind of lights and what sort of filters, or *gels*, they need. Gels are a transparent material used to change the way a light looks. They come in different colors or materials, and each has a different effect on the way the light looks as it is filtered through the gel. Depending on the scene, the light might need to be harsh, like a fluorescent bulb, or soft, like a candle. Maybe it's a scene inside a club, and the light needs to be blue and purple. Gaffers use gels and light reflectors to accomplish all these different looks. They generally aren't afraid of heights, since many of the lights used on a film set are positioned up high and require a ladder to set up and adjust.

Not only do they need to create each lighting setup; gaffers also change the lighting from scene to scene, which means they've got to figure out how to position all the lights, then quickly change them as soon as the scene is finished being shot. On top of all this, gaffers are responsible for making sure the electrical setups on the set are safe. Their crews run all the cables and wires and make sure they're taped to the floor and won't cause any trips or accidents. Being a gaffer is a lot of responsibility! But it is really creative, too. Gaffers have an eye for lighting and are fantastic at figuring out how to achieve all sorts of lighting effects.

GAFFER CAROLINA SCHMIDTHOLSTEIN DESCRIBES HER JOB AS CREATING "MOODS WITH LIGHTS AND SHADOWS."

So, while the gaffer and her crew are working to light the scene, any other lighting, camera, or electrical equipment is set up by the *grips*, technicians who are responsible for setting up and *striking* (taking down) such equipment. Some of the grips might help the gaffers by assembling the stands and rigs for the lights, while others might

work with the camera crew to set up the rigging for the cameras. Grips are basically professional put-it-together-ers and pack-it-away-ers.

Most films have a whole crew of grips to help set up and then break down quickly and efficiently. The woman in charge of the grip crew is called the *key grip*. Then the second-in-command to either the key grip or gaffer is called a *best boy*, but clearly, that is an outdated term that needs to be changed. Women and nonbinary people make really great best boys, too.

WHENEVER YOU SEE THE WORD "KEY" IN FRONT OF ANY FILM CREW POSITION, IT MEANS THAT PERSON IS IN CHARGE.

Grips are strong, reliable women who are able to run around all day and handle doing some of the hardest physical labor on a film set. It takes a lot of stamina to be a grip! They've got to load equipment out of the trucks early in the morning, set it up, strike it and move it around all day, then load it back into the truck at night. Gaffers and grips both wear heavy tool belts and thick gloves, and you can bet that grips have pretty nice biceps.

If the camera is going to be moving at all—like mounted on a car, for example—it'll be the grips who set the rigging up to attach the camera. However, when it's time to start rolling, the grips and gaffers hand things off to the camera crew.

Alright, now the scene is set and it is time to roll the cameras!

During the shoot for the opening scene, in which Sasha hangs out in her room, waiting for her friends to arrive, she wears what the costume designer put together for her: green Dr. Martens boots, leggings with lightning bolts, and a jean jacket. There could even be enamel pins of lipstick tubes, eyeliners, and all sorts of makeup tools to stick into the front lapels of the jacket. With that costume, Sasha definitely looks ready to apply some killer makeup and kick some zombie butt.

THE OPENING SCENES FOR SASHA VERSUS ZOMBIES MIGHT BE SHOT FIRST, BUT IT IS IMPORTANT TO KNOW THAT MOST FILMS ARE SHOT TOTALLY OUT OF SEQUENCE! THE ORDER IN WHICH SCENES ARE SHOT DEPENDS ON MANY VARIABLES, INCLUDING ACTOR AND LOCATION AVAILABILITY, AND WEATHER CONDITIONS IF THE SHOOT IS OUTSIDE.

The actress playing Sasha is standing in the middle of the set, under the carefully arranged lights, ready to rock and roll. The director is standing with the DP near the camera, but the director doesn't usually look through the camera directly. Instead something called a *video village* is set up, with monitors showing what the camera is capturing, so that the DP and director can see what's going on together. It's useful because it means that multiple people can see what the camera is shooting at the same time.

The person who actually operates the camera is called, appropriately, the *camera operator*. She's the one who captures the shots. After making sure the camera is set up properly, she handles the camera when it's rolling.

> IF THE DP HERSELF IS ALSO THE CAMERA OPERATOR,
> THEN SHE'LL BE CALLED A CINEMATOGRAPHER.

Camera operators obviously love cameras, but they are also great at communicating and collaborating, since they work so closely with directors and DPs, plus they have an eye for figuring out the right composition of a scene. Being a camera operator is a great way to work toward being a director of photography, too.

However, operating the camera is a big job, so even the camera operator gets some help from the *first assistant camera*. Her job is to help set the camera up, change out the lenses, and keep the shot in focus. In fact, a first assistant camera is sometimes called a *focus puller* because she pulls the shot into focus. This is an important job. It'd be terrible to shoot a whole scene and find out that the footage of it was blurry!

Focus pullers are meticulous and very, well, focused. They measure the distance between the camera lens and the object or person in the shot that the director wants to be in focus. That measurement will help them *pull the focus* by adjusting the camera so that the shot is clear and sharp.

You know that fun black-and-white clapper that you always see in movies about movies? It's the job of the *second assistant camera* to clap it. That clapper is also known as a *slate*, and, on top of making a satisfying noise, it's an essential filmmaking tool. In fact, the noise the slate makes when the second assistant camera snaps it shut helps the editor sync up the audio and the video, and the information written on the front helps keep track of what scene is being shot and how many takes have been needed so far to shoot the scene. While the first assistant camera works more with the camera directly, the second assistant camera works more in front of the camera, because she is the one who writes on the slate, tapes down marks on the floor to show the actors where to stand in relation to the camera, and helps the AD keep track of everything that has been shot that day.

So, now you know that movies definitely aren't just shot with one person holding a camera. Instead, there is a whole talented crew behind the camera making sure everything is in focus and going according to plan.

With the camera in place for the visuals, what about sound?

Even though movies are obviously a visual medium, sound is also incredibly crucial for the audience's experience. Just like with the camera, there are talented people on the sound team making sure all the sound is captured well.

The woman responsible for recording the sound on the set, whether in a studio or on a location, is called the *sound mixer*. She's also responsible for making sure the sound is balanced and, well, sounds good. The sound mixer makes sure that one actor isn't quieter than another actor and that there are no weird background noises. Sometimes, she'll even visit the location or studio beforehand to make sure that there won't be any problems with the sound. For instance, the location might be near an airport, or a loud highway, or a high school football stadium. It would be annoying to have a bunch of booing and cheering in the background of the zombie fight scenes at Sasha's high school, so the sound mixer needs to know what she might be dealing with ahead of filming.

After she assesses where the movie will be shot, the sound mixer then assesses what sort of recording equipment she'll need. Normally, actors have a hidden battery pack and microphone clipped somewhere in their costume, which are called *lavalier microphones*, or "lav mics" for short. The sound mixer will be able to hear everything at her station on set and also give headphones to the director, producer, and anyone else who needs to hear what's going on in the scene.

THE FIRST WOMAN TO EVER BE NOMINATED FOR AN OSCAR FOR SOUND MIXING WAS ANNA BEHLMER, FOR BRAVEHEART IN 1996. SHE WENT ON TO BE NOMINATED TEN MORE TIMES! SHE TOLD THE HOLLYWOOD REPORTER IN 2018, "PEOPLE THINK THAT IT'S VERY TECHNICAL, WHICH IT IS, BUT IT'S REALLY AN ART FORM. TO BALANCE A SOUNDSCAPE AGAINST IMAGES WITH DIALOGUE AND MUSIC AND SOUND EFFECTS—IT'S ALL SUPPORTING THE STORY."

In addition to being responsible for recording all the actors' dialogue on the set, she also records what's called *wild sound*, which aren't noises that sound really silly. Wild sound means any nonhuman sound that happens at the location that the director might want to incorporate into the film, which could be anything from the sound of the wind or the ocean to birds chirping.

A good sound mixer should know a lot about sound quality and audio engineering. If you're picky about the type of audio files you vlisten to or love getting nerdy about speakers and headphone quality, this job might be fun for you! Being a sound assistant or trainee is a great way to get started in the world of movie sound work.

The sound mixer works closely with the *boom operator*. If you've ever watched behind-the-scenes clips of movies, you've probably seen someone holding what looks like a furry animal on a stick over the actor's heads. That furry thing on a long stick is the *boom microphone*, the long stick is the *boom pole*, and the person who has to position it above the people talking is the boom operator. The furry

part is called a *blimp*, and it's used to protect the microphone from any unwanted background noise and make sure that it doesn't pick up the sound of the wind. It is tough to be a boom operator because she must keep the boom mic close enough to the actor to pick up their voices well but far enough away that it doesn't get caught in the camera frame.

You might be thinking, why does someone have to hold the boom mic during the whole scene, instead of attaching it to a stand or something? Well, that's because the boom mic is sensitive and needs to be close to the actors. If they're moving around a scene, even in a small bedroom, the sound quality is best if someone is holding it and making small adjustments and moving around with the actor. Yes, boom operators have very strong arms. They also assist the sound mixer and clip the microphones and battery packs to the actors.

Working as a boom operator is like being a sound assistant, a fantastic way to start working in the movie sound business and a fantastic way to work on your triceps.

So, there's the whole camera crew, sound crew, director, assistant director, DP, and maybe even the producer on set, all ready to go. Film sets can be crowded places! The actors are on their marks and ready to say their lines.

Instead of yelling, "Lights, camera, action!" the director or assistant director first yells, "QUIET ON THE SET!" to make sure everyone around knows that they're about to start shooting. Then, she yells, "Roll sound!" to make sure the sound mixer and boom operator have the sound going. Then, she yells, "Roll camera!" to make sure the camera crew has the camera rolling. Then, she yells, "Marker!" or "Slate!" to have the second camera assistant clap the slate in front of the camera.

Then, the command everyone's been preparing for . . . "Action!"

Finally, you're shooting a movie!

A. Flip to the next page.

*DAY
ONE HUNDRED
AND SIXTY*

ZOMBIELAND

MOST FILM SHOOTS LAST FOR ABOUT A MONTH, WITH DAYS OFF on the weekends. Of course, the bigger the movie, the longer the shoot will be. The 2021 Marvel film *Eternals*, directed by Chloé Zhao, took eighty-two days to shoot!

Even after the first week of shooting, there is already a lot of digital footage, which means that someone needs to keep track of it. That's where a couple of indispensable members of the production crew come in, logging what's going on both in front of the camera and behind it.

Keeping track of things in front of the camera is the *script supervisor*. Details are the name of her game. Her whole responsibility is to keep track of all the specifics in the script and in the previous scenes. She is the queen of *continuity*, which means that all the details of a scene—what the actors are wearing, what the actors say, the weather outside, how the props move, and so on—stay consistent. She watches each take closely and makes meticulous notes, so that if something needs to be reshot later, the director or assistant director can refer to her notes and make sure everything matches up.

During each scene, the script supervisor will also check the scene against the latest version of the script and make sure no actions or dialogue are forgotten or missed. She also keeps track of anything that has been added to the script. Sometimes, actors improvise and say or do something that isn't in the script—whether by accident or on purpose—and if the director likes it and decides to keep it that way, it's the script supervisor's responsibility to make a note of that.

> THE FAMOUS "YOU'RE GOING TO NEED A BIGGER BOAT" LINE FROM JAWS WAS TOTALLY IMPROVISED, AND IT WORKED SO WELL THAT THE FILMMAKERS DECIDED TO KEEP IT. SCRIPT SUPERVISOR CHARLSIE BRYANT WAS THE WOMAN WHO MADE A NOTE OF IT!

The script supervisor also works with the DP to keep track of how each scene is shot and lit. She makes notes of what camera lenses were used, what angle the camera was shooting from, and what sort of lights the crew set up for the scene. That way, if a scene needs to be reshot—which often does happen—the camera crew can set everything up exactly how it was. Obviously, script supervisors have expert-level observation skills and are extremely detail oriented. They're detail masters, not to mention amazing note takers.

BEING A SCRIPT SUPERVISOR IS A JOB THAT COULD TAKE YOU TO ANY GENRE OF MOVIE. SCRIPT SUPERVISOR MARY CYBULSKI HAS WORKED ON MOVIES FROM THE ROMANTIC ETERNAL SUNSHINE OF THE SPOTLESS MIND TO THE FANTASTIC LAST AIRBENDER TO THE ADVENTUROUS LIFE OF PI.

After nearly two weeks of hard work and shooting (with Sundays off), the production team for *Sasha Versus Zombies* is making great progress. They've moved on from the early scenes in Sasha's house and are shooting the scenes where Sasha and her friends run through the neighborhood with hungry zombies on their tails.

In one shot of Sasha and her friends running down the street, Sasha holds her baseball bat, all bloody with zombie guts. The director wants to get a shot of the scene from a different angle, so the lighting, grip, and camera crews move all the lights, equipment, and cameras to a different setup. They shoot the scene again, but this time, the actress playing Sasha forgets to grab her baseball bat. It's the script supervisor's job to catch those mistakes. The scene would look weird if Sasha had her baseball bat in one shot, and then a second later, the bat was gone. Just like it would look weird if Sasha grabbed the wrong prop. It wouldn't do to have her holding a perfectly clean bat in the same scene that she crushed some zombies with it.

Before shooting, the script supervisor will also do a pass through the script to flag any continuity problems. Maybe one of Sasha's friends says that they are allergic to peanuts later on in the movie, but there's a scene in the beginning where they're eating a peanut butter and jelly sandwich. It's the script supervisor's job to catch those little inconsistencies before they make it on camera.

Keeping track of things behind the camera is the *digital imaging technician*, or DIT.

It wasn't until the 2000s that movies began to be shot digitally. Up until then, movies were shot using real film, and the process of filmmaking was a bit different. Nowadays, just like with still cameras, it's mostly digital.

Shooting digital is much less expensive and gives more flexibility to directors. Instead of having to haul around heavy canisters of physical film, camera crews use tiny, light memory cards. You can fit millions of hours of footage onto all the memory cards that could fit into one film canister. Because of that, directors can be freer with how much they shoot and don't have to worry about running out of film.

With new digital film cameras to operate and digital film storage to manage, a new job was born: the DIT. The digital imaging technician works with the DP (yes, there are a lot of acronyms and initialisms in the movie world) to manage the digital image that the camera is capturing. She's a tech wizard.

During the shoot, the DIT sits in the video village and monitors what is being shot. She makes sure that nothing is off, like the exposure, the brightness, or the colors. If during yesterday's shoot, everything looked bright and fully saturated with colors, but today the picture is coming in darker and less saturated, it's the DIT's job to adjust the equipment until it looks right again. She also keeps an eye out for any unwanted reflections or shadows. Maybe the light shining off an actor's glasses is causing a weird-looking glare, or there is a shadow of one of the crew members eating a snack in the background of the shot. It's the DIT's job to spot these kinds of problems in the video village monitor and point them out.

Another super important part of the DIT's job is data management. You know how iPhones and computers need to be regularly backed up so that in case something happens, all their data will be saved? The same thing happens for movies. It's critical for the DIT to regularly back up the digital footage so that if there's some sort of error, the scenes don't have to be shot again. You can see just how much goes into shooting a movie and how many people need to be there to help. It's a huge pain in the butt to reshoot!

The DIT is also responsible for taking all the data and making sure it gets to the post-production crew (you'll meet them later). At the end of each shooting day, the raw, unedited footage is called the *dailies*. The DIT organizes, backs up, and stores all the dailies on hard drives that will be safely transferred to the folks in post-production.

~~~~~~~~

If this sounds like a lot of work, that's because it is! It means that the whole team responsible for making the movie can work up quite an appetite.

Most shooting days are between twelve and sixteen hours long. With so much to do, a film crew doesn't have time to run out to order something from Chipotle on their lunch breaks, and there are simply too many people on a set for a production assistant to run out to pick up food for everyone. That's a lot of burritos for one person to carry.

Food is so important to a film crew that there are two teams responsible for feeding everyone. The first team is called *craft services*, or "crafty" for short, and they handle the most important thing in the world: snacks.

Instead of setting out hot, cooked meals, crafty maintains a table (or if it's a big production, lots of tables) covered in water, drinks, and snacks of all kinds. The food and beverages at craft services are available all day, at all times. They're called craft services because they're technically meant to provide snacks for all the "crafts" on set, such as the grips, the gaffer, the camera crew—all the craftspeople who are working long, hard hours and might need food on the go. But everyone on set—from the actors to the production assistants—can come over to crafty to get something to eat. Sometimes, a crafty person will bring snacks to crew members who are so busy that they can't stop to visit the table.

As you can imagine, this is a critical job. Having access to something good to eat and plenty of beverages for hydration can make the difference between a cranky, tired crew that is struggling and a happy, energetic crew that is kicking some butt. Keeping everything stocked and fresh is the top priority for craft services, and a good crafty team makes sure to provide food and drinks for all sorts of dietary restrictions and tastes.

The other food-related team on a film set is *catering*, the folks who provide hot, sit-down meals. Generally, the rule is that the film crew gets to have a sit-down meal every six hours. Depending on how long that day's shoot is, that could mean breakfast, lunch, and dinner. But usually, it's just lunch and dinner. Each meal break is between thirty and sixty minutes long and gives the entire film crew a chance to rest.

The types of food that catering and craft services have vary depending on the budget of the movie. If it's a low-budget film, the catering is probably going to be mostly pizza and sandwiches. But on a high-budget movie, the food can get really fancy and with a lot of variety from day to day. Taco trucks, sushi, fresh pasta—you name it!

Because it takes so long for the actors to get into their costumes, hair, and makeup, they don't take everything off just to eat lunch. Most actors will get wrapped in a bathrobe and sent right over to catering. On a movie like *Sasha Versus Zombies*, those in zombie makeup are given long straws to drink through to make sure they don't mess up their makeup too much.

Even with bathrobes and straws, actors usually come back from lunch needing some touch-ups to their look. That's where the *set costumer* comes in.

On a set, she's responsible for making sure all the costumes look right. Straightening ties, rolling a lint brush over a dress, wiping mustard off a sleeve—the set costumer makes sure that everyone looks good . . . or at least looks like they did before they went to lunch.

The set costumer assists the costume designer during pre-production, but once the movie starts shooting, the designer's job is mostly finished. It's the set costumer who comes to set every day.

Of course, the set costumer doesn't just bring herself—she also transports all the costumes. Making sure there is a designated person in each department—whether it's the costume department, art department, or camera department—who is in charge of bringing whatever is needed to set each day is really, really important. Having everyone assume someone else is bringing the costumes, the props, or the camera lenses can lead to huge delays, especially if the movie is shooting on a location that's hours and hours away from the production office. You wouldn't want to be running around the zombified high school first thing in the morning, looking for the props you need for the *Sasha Versus Zombies* scene you're about to shoot.

So, not only does the set costumer bring all costumes and accessories (hats, gloves, etc.) to set, but she must transport them all properly as well, so they don't get crushed or wrinkled. She can't throw them all in a bag and go because all the costumes must be hung up or folded. (They're not like the dirty laundry on the floor in your room.)

Once she gets to the set and unpacks all the costumes, then she makes sure the right actors get the right costumes. The set costumer also instructs the actors on the proper care of the costume, which is usually something along the lines of "please don't rip this or get ketchup on it." In the costume department trailer or area, she creates a spot for actors to leave their costumes at the end of the day and a spot to leave any costume that needs repairs or cleaning.

Keeping track of each piece of each costume and who is wearing what means that she needs to be very organized. Most set costumers keep a log book of which actor wore which costume on which day for which scene. This helps the script supervisor keep track of continuity and helps ensure the right costumes are worn in the right scenes. It also means the right *versions* of each costume. It would look pretty silly for Sasha to be wearing the clean version of her costume after she just beat up a bunch of bloody, gory zombies.

If any of the costumes have been rented, a log book also helps the set costumer keep track of what needs to be cleaned and returned to the costume warehouse. Losing or damaging a costume that was rented could cost a production a lot of money! The log book also helps to track any on-set changes. Maybe right before the cameras started rolling, one of the actors playing Sasha's friends decided that their character would roll their sleeves up. The script supervisor and set costumer keep track of this change for future scenes.

Costumes constantly need to be repaired, and having great sewing skills is very helpful for this job. Depending on how big the film is and how big the budget is, the set costumer might have assistants, tailors, seamstresses, and even a shopper to help her. So, while the costume designer works on the designs of the costumes before the film starts, it's the set costumer who works on the costumes themselves while the movie is filming. They're both great jobs if you love clothes!

STUNT DOUBLE, TOIL AND TROUBLE

I N ANY MOVIE THAT FEATURES ACTION AND FIGHT SEQUENCES, there's going to be a lot of punching. And falling. And stuff flying everywhere.

Does it look extremely cool? Absolutely yes.

Does it also require a lot of work to make sure that everyone is extremely safe? Also yes.

Stunt performers are the unsung heroes of the film world. They're the ones doing all that awesome stuff on screen. *Stunts* are physical feats that are usually daring or dangerous and require a special skill, like horseback riding, acrobatics, or shooting. A stunt performer must be extremely athletic to pull them off. She should be able to fight and use martial arts, swim and dive, ride horses and motorcycles, and most importantly . . . fall. Being able to fall without hurting yourself is one of the most useful (and used) skills in stunts. Next time you watch a movie, pay attention to how often the stunts end in a carefully coordinated fall, whether it's from a horse, from a helicopter, or just on the sidewalk. Often this is in action or horror movies, but any genre of film can call for stunts, especially comedy!

> STUNT PERFORMERS ARE CALLED STUNT DOUBLES WHEN THEY ARE MADE UP TO LOOK LIKE THE ACTOR WHOSE CHARACTER IS DOING THE STUNT AND TAKE THEIR PLACE. SOME ACTORS DO THEIR OWN STUNTS (LIKE GAL GADOT AND CHARLIZE THERON), BUT USUALLY A STUNT DOUBLE IS USED.

The name of the game in stunts is always safety. Although it's important that the scene looks cool, it's far more important that everyone is always safe. A scene might require numerous takes, which means a stunt must be well planned so it can be done over and over again without injuring the stunt performers. That's part of why learning to fall is so crucial! A stunt performer won't be falling out of a window just once but many times. Even though real glass isn't used—the "glass" in movies is made from a thin, see-through sugar that is cheap to make, very brittle, and shatters easily—if the stunt isn't well planned, the performer might get hurt.

Stunt performers are strong, flexible, and creative. They can't just do the stunt; they've really got to sell it, just like actors need to sell their performances so that they feel real—especially if they're a stunt double. They've got to carefully observe the movements of the actor they're doubling and make the stunt look as if it's the actor doing it. Stunt work is art work. But if the stunt performers are performing the stunts, who is the person planning them?

The *stunt coordinator* is the woman responsible for coordinating and planning all the stunts. She works closely with the director to figure out what stunts are needed and how to make them happen safely. She'll design them and create action sequences that can be broken down into parts.

MONIQUE GANDERTON WORKED AS MARVEL'S FIRST-EVER FEMALE STUNT COORDINATOR ON AVENGERS: ENDGAME. SHE COORDINATED FIGHTS AND STUNTS FOR THE BIG BATTLE IN A FILM FEATURING THE MOST SUPERHEROES EVER SHOWN ON SCREEN!

Besides the fun stuff like choreographing stunts, the stunt coordinator handles the expenses and budget for the stunt department. She keeps track of how much money she's spending on gear, how much she's paying her performers, and how many hours everyone in her department is working. Many stunt coordinators start out as stunt performers and eventually decide they want to be on the other side of the camera. Being a stunt coordinator requires excellent leadership skills and an expert-level knowledge of stunts, fighting, and weapons built up over years of stunt work.

So, there might be a scene in *Sasha Versus Zombies* where Sasha and her friends are running through her neighborhood to escape a horde of the undead who were not fooled by Sasha's zombie makeup, and the group ends up on the roof of one of Sasha's neighbor's houses. In the script, the friends jump from the roof to a tree that is next to the house, then jump down from the tree, battle a lone zombie at the base, and run to a bunch of bicycles lying in the backyard. While pedaling as fast as they can, Sasha and her friends ride down the street and hit a few zombies with their makeshift weapons. It is an exciting, action-packed scene!

To bring this scene to life, the stunt coordinator breaks the whole scene down into individual stunts:

- Jumping into the tree from the roof
- Jumping onto the ground from the tree
- Zombie fight

- Running to the bicycles and hopping on
- Riding down the street while whacking zombies on the way

Then the stunt coordinator figures out which stunt performers and doubles are needed for the scene. Four stunt doubles for Sasha and her three friends, and then at least three or four stunt performers to play the zombies. The stunt coordinator hires her own stunt crew and tells the producer what kind of equipment she needs for each stunt throughout the movie. Stunts often require gear like pads to protect body parts, cushioned mats to land on, and springboards to jump from. The stunt coordinator also works with the prop master (and if there are a lot of weapons and guns on a film, the *armorer*, whose job it is to handle all the weapons) to figure out which prop weapons are needed.

LAFAYE BAKER BECAME THE FIRST BLACK WOMAN TO BE A STUNT COORDINATOR FOR TELEVISION WHEN SHE WAS HIRED FOR THE SHOW SISTER, SISTER! SHE IS THE FOUNDER OF THE ACTION ICON AWARDS, WHICH HONORS WOMEN IN STUNT WORK.

Once she has the crew and gear she needs, the stunt coordinator starts designing and choreographing the stunts. She has her performers practice them over and over until they look great on camera and are perfectly safe for everyone involved (not just the performers but the crew around them). Soon . . . boom! You've got an action-packed scene.

For the first stunt, the stunt coordinator needs the four stunt doubles of Sasha and her friends and a big, cushioned mat to land on. Because it is too dangerous for the stunt doubles to actually jump from a roof into a tree, the stunt coordinator works with the director to break it down into shots. One shot could be the stunt doubles from behind (so their faces are hidden) jumping from the roof. When they jump, they land on a soft mat on the ground. But thanks to some smart work in the editing room later, the shot with the jump will cut directly to a shot of the teens sitting in the branches of the tree so it looks like they just landed. Movie magic!

After the two jumps—from the roof and from the tree—are shot, then it's time for a zombie fight! That's when the *fight coordinator* is called in. She is the one who choreographs and helps direct combat sequences. She doesn't work on any of the other

stunts, just the fights, and it is her job to make sure the zombie fights in *Sasha Versus Zombies* look believable (well, as believable as zombie fights can be) and keep the stunt performers safe.

She's extremely knowledgeable about all sorts of fighting styles, even old-timey historical ones. Karate, boxing, fencing, wrestling . . . you name it, she can kick your butt in it. It's her job to match up the fighting with the kind of movie that is being filmed. It wouldn't make sense for Sasha and her friends to wrestle the zombies like Roman gladiators, so the fight coordinator has to figure out how a bunch of suburban American teenagers would fight zombies. Probably with a lot of regular ol' punching and kicking.

Once she has done her research and is ready for the scene, the fight coordinator works with the director, the DP, the camera crew, and the stunt doubles to *block* the scene. Blocking a scene is basically just figuring out how everything and everyone is going to move. Where will the actors move from and to? How will the camera move with them, if at all?

This is when the storyboards really come in handy because now the director can show what the scene looks like in her head to the fight coordinator, who can do her best to make it happen in front of the camera. Everyone works together to decide what looks best, with the director making the final call, as long as what she wants is approved as safe by the fight coordinator.

So, the team discusses and brainstorms different ideas for when Sasha and her friends jump down from the tree and start fighting the zombie hanging out at the base. There are so many cool ways to shoot a scene like this!

Depending on what the crew decides, the camera department can hire a special crew member with specialized gear to make the camera move along with Sasha. Or, the camera will be stationary, while the stunt crew has their own special crew member build a rig to make the zombie fly through the air after getting pummeled.

What do you think would look cooler?

A. **Make that zombie fly!**

   Continue to the next page.

B. **You want cool camera moves.**

   Flip to page 76.

IT'S RAINING ZOMBIES

ALRIGHT, FLYING ZOMBIES, COMING RIGHT UP!

While the stunt coordinator designs the stunts, the *stunt rigger* designs the system of ropes, pulleys, and harnesses that makes the more elaborate stunts happen. Whether it's sliding under a speeding car or tumbling off a cliff, the stunt rigger creates a system that keeps the stunt performer safe and the stunt looking cool.

STUNT PROFESSIONAL NANCY THURSTON WORKED ON MOVIES LIKE TITANIC AND CHARLIE'S ANGELS, AS WELL AS ON TELEVISION. SHE WAS THE STUNT RIGGER FOR THE ENTIRE ORIGINAL RUN OF THE SHOW CHARMED. NANCY MADE A LOT OF WITCHES FLY THROUGH THE AIR!

After going through the script and storyboards and assessing all of the stunts that the director wants to do, the stunt coordinator figures out which stunts call for a stunt rigger. The stunt rigger works with the stunt coordinator to decide what sort of gear and safety equipment are needed to achieve the stunt. Her job involves a lot of problem solving and reverse engineering. A stunt rigger will often work backward from where the stunt performer is supposed to end up, then make sketches of possible rigs and pulley systems before she begins to build. If it's a big movie with a lot of elaborate stunt rigs, the stunt rigger will have a team of riggers who report to her, and she'll be called the *stunt rigger coordinator*.

As you can imagine, there's a lot of trust involved in being a stunt rigger. If she's not doing her job correctly, someone could get hurt. Many stunt riggers start out their careers in rock climbing, where they learn how to belay, tie knots, use different kinds of rope and harnesses, and assess situations for safety.

Let's say the director for *Sasha Versus Zombies* decides that she doesn't want the zombie to get punched by Sasha in the backyard. Instead, she wants the zombie to climb up the tree, get kicked in the head by Sasha, then land on a nearby trampoline before flying over the fence. This is a much more complicated stunt than what was originally in the script, but after a chat, the stunt coordinator and stunt rigger decide they can make it happen.

To make the director's flying zombie dream come true, the stunt rigger suggests they film the scene in segments like these:

- The zombie getting kicked and falling
- The zombie landing on the trampoline
- The zombie flying over the fence

Once the crew is all on the same page, the stunt performer playing the zombie gets snugly fitted into a harness, attached to a rope, attached to a pulley, attached to a rig made of steel beams. Underneath her ragged zombie costume is some cleverly concealed padding. After some test runs, the stunt team is ready to shoot the zombie getting kicked and falling onto the trampoline—the stunt performer actually falls onto a big, squishy landing pad on the ground.

The first take looks perfect! The stunt performer lets out a scary zombie growl as she is mock-kicked and a big howl as she falls to the landing pad. Even if the director gets a perfect take, she'll usually ask for a second take for safety, which doesn't mean what you might think. When it comes to shooting, saying "for safety" means even though the take you just got looks great, it's handy to have a second take, just in case something was wrong with the first shot that no one noticed.

However, while the crew is setting up for the second take, the stunt performer has to run to the bathroom. The stunt rigger doesn't double-check the harness when the performer gets back into it and the straps are a little loose. During the second take . . . BONK! The stunt performer hits her head on a branch.

Oh no! That means it's time to visit the *set medic*!

A. Continue to the next page.

PARA-MEDICAL ACTIVITY

DESPITE ALL THE SAFETY PRECAUTIONS, ACCIDENTS ARE PRETTY common on a film set. Cuts, bruises, concussions, broken limbs—all sorts of trouble can happen.

A set medic is a registered nurse or a paramedic who is always on set and attends to any health issues that arise. She's the first responder if anything, small or serious, happens during the shoot. A set medic has her own first aid kits that she brings along to every movie she works on, and along with basic bandages and alcohol pads, she also keeps supplies like epi pens, in case anyone has an allergic reaction.

If she can't treat an injury on the set, it is the set medic's responsibility to organize a trip to the hospital. Before shooting begins, she figures out the nearest hospital to whatever studio or location the movie is being shot at. She has the phone number for that hospital on hand and knows exactly how long it takes to get there—important information to have during an emergency!

Many set medics start out as lifeguards or EMTs, and they have excellent first aid skills and must be fast thinkers. Safety is always the top priority on a film shoot, but it's nice for the crew (especially the stunt crew) to know that someone is on hand to take care of any injuries quickly.

Back on the *Sasha Versus Zombies* set, the set medic assesses this zombified stunt performer's head and makes sure that she has no cuts, scrapes, a concussion, or any other serious head injuries. If she can't find anything wrong and the stunt performer feels okay, the set medic will give the thumbs up, and the performer can head back to the scene. Even if there is no visible injury after an accident, it's always a good idea to pause the production and have the set medic check things out, just in case.

Whenever she's not attending to an injury, the set medic is part of the team that assesses the stunts to make sure everything looks safe. The set medic might notice something that the stunt crew doesn't, such as a harness rubbing on a stunt performer in a spot that might cause a blister or a part of the set that might be a risk for splinters or cuts.

After the set medic gives the A-okay, the shoot can resume, and you are ready to get back to fighting zombies.

A. Flip to page 78.

DROP DEAD STEAD

COOL CAMERA MOVES, COMING RIGHT UP!
   Whenever you see a shot in a movie where the camera is moving but the scene doesn't look shaky, it's probably because it was captured with either a *steadicam* or a camera *dolly*.

A steadicam is a specialized camera rig that is worn like a backpack and stabilizes the camera so the *steadicam operator* can walk around without the footage looking like a shaky home movie. Just like other members of the camera department, the steadicam operator collaborates closely with the director and DP so she can capture the exact shot they're looking for. While wearing the body harness that the steadicam is attached to, she must walk in an extremely fluid motion to help the rig capture an extra-smooth shot. A steadicam operator is similar to a camera operator, but hers is a much more physical job because instead of adjusting the camera stand, she *is* the camera stand.

> HAVE YOU EVER SEEN THE ULTRA-SCARY MOVIE THE SHINING? THE SPOOKY SHOTS WHERE THE CAMERA FOLLOWS DANNY WHILE HE RIDES THROUGH THE CORRIDORS OF THE OVERLOOK HOTEL ON HIS TRICYCLE WERE ACHIEVED WITH A STEADICAM!

Many steadicam operators begin their careers as camera operators. For them, it is extremely helpful to have a lot of photography and choreography know-how, and they have to be able to walk fluidly without stumbling. Being graceful definitely comes in handy if you want to be a steadicam operator!

Directors usually use a steadicam when they want to capture a moving shot that isn't in a straight line, such as someone walking around a corner or a terrified character running in zig-zags across a field. If the director wants to capture a moving shot that's happening in a straight line, she usually uses a camera dolly. (No Barbies involved.) Putting the camera on a dolly is great if a director wants a shot that is precise and repeatable.

A dolly is just a wheeled cart that a camera gets mounted to. Most dollies are extremely heavy—we're talking five hundred pounds!—which is good for keeping the camera steady, but it also means that a special grip is needed to operate it, known as a *dolly grip*. Most dollies move along a *track* that is laid down before filming starts, just like a huge, incredibly expensive toy train. While the camera is rolling, the dolly grip is the woman operating and moving it along the track as fast or slow as the director wants. Sometimes, the dolly is big enough that the camera operator sits on top of it during the shot so she can monitor the camera as it moves. The dolly grip is responsible for both laying down the track and striking it once the shot is captured.

> SHOTS ACHIEVED WITH A CAMERA ON A DOLLY TRACK ARE GREAT FOR ACTION MOVIES. IN INDIANA JONES THE SHOT WHERE INDY RUNS THROUGH THE TEMPLE CHAMBER AWAY FROM A ROLLING BOULDER WAS CAPTURED THIS WAY.

Great dolly grips are strong, consistent, and fantastic communicators. When you're rolling a camera operator along a track, you've got to be!

Ultimately, for *Sasha Versus Zombies*, the director decides to use a steadicam to capture a shot of Sasha running toward a zombie climbing over her neighbor's fence. The steadicam operator works with the DP and director on how exactly she moves through the scene.

Her mark is at the base of the tree, close to where Sasha lands as she jumps out of the branches. The shot would begin with Sasha's green Doc Martens hitting the ground and follow quickly along as Sasha bashes the zombie at the base of the tree then runs toward a zombie crawling over the wooden slats of the fence. The steadicam operator must follow Sasha at a steady pace without stumbling or bumping the actress with the camera rig. When the shot is captured, the quick, close movement of the camera makes the scene feel extra intense and heart pounding!

If Sasha is going to annihilate the zombie crawling over the fence with her baseball bat, she might hit the fence itself and make some wood chips go flying. You're going to need some help pulling that effect off on camera.

A. Flip to the next page.

THE SFX-ORCIST

WHEN YOU HEAR THE WORDS "SPECIAL EFFECTS," YOU PROBABLY think back to our pre-production visit to the special effects makeup shop, where the SFX artist created the zombie makeups. Those artists create special effects that are applied onto actors. But there are many more types of special effects that go into a film.

A good way to think of special effects is through the four elements: fire, wind, earth, or water. Fog, explosions, and smoke to rain, earthquakes, and snow—all these effects are part of the responsibility of the *special effects supervisor*, sometimes called the *special effects coordinator*, and she is responsible for making any special effects happen in a safe and spectacular manner.

By now, you can probably guess the process she goes through to get started. First, she meets with the director, production designer, and art director to look through the script and the shot list before deciding which special effects she is going to need and how they are going to look with the rest of the film. The SFX supervisor also has to figure out what sort of gear she needs. Does she need a fog machine? Smoke powder? A rain rig? A snowmaker? If there are a lot of stunts in a film that involve special effects, such as a stunt performer jumping through a window or rolling across a fire, the SFX supervisor collaborates with the stunt team as well.

THIS FAR INTO PRODUCTION, YOU CAN SEE HOW BIG OF A JOB BEING A DIRECTOR IS! THINK OF ALL THE DEPARTMENT HEADS THAT YOU'VE MET THAT SHE MUST COLLABORATE WITH!

After she figures out what kinds of special effects the film requires, she plans how each effect will be executed. This way she knows how many *special effects technicians* she needs to hire to be on her crew. Before shooting starts, the SFX supervisor and her team often test the special effects to make sure they work and, more importantly, to make sure they are safe. Special effects are usually *manual*, which means done by hand, or *mechanical*, which means done by machine, and both types need to be tested before they're used during filming. For example, it would be a disaster, and would cost the film time, if the snow machine didn't work for a scene where characters are supposed to be catching flakes on their tongues. It is also important that the special effects team uses environmentally friendly and nontoxic materials to create their effects—especially if an actor has to catch that special effect on their tongue!

SPECIAL EFFECTS SUPERVISOR MAGGIE ANNE GOLL HAS WORKED ON MOVIES SUCH AS BILL & TED FACE THE MUSIC AND THE FOREVER PURGE, AND HER ADVICE TO FOLKS STARTING OUT IN THE SPECIAL EFFECTS INDUSTRY (AS TOLD TO THE LOS ANGELES TIMES IN 2021) IS "LISTEN AND LEARN . . . [T]HERE ARE SO MANY WAYS TO DO SOMETHING RIGHT, AND IT NEVER HURTS TO LEARN A NEW WAY."

Most special effects supervisors and technicians start out working as prop makers in a prop shop, where they learn skills, such as woodworking or making artificial glass, and then move on to work in SFX shops. Others start out as apprentices in SFX shops and are trained by special effects supervisors. Women who become good SFX technicians and supervisors have fantastic creative vision and are focused on safety. It's one thing to say you want an explosion in a scene, but it's another to be able to visualize how that explosion will look on camera, plus figure out how to execute it safely, before you even test it out.

ANIMATRONICS, MINIATURES, MONSTER MAKEUPS, FIERY EXPLOSIONS, AND CAR CHASES ALL FALL UNDER THE UMBRELLA OF SPECIAL EFFECTS. THESE ARE ALL DIFFERENT BRANCHES OF PRACTICAL EFFECTS (REMEMBER: EFFECTS DONE IN REAL LIFE) IN FRONT OF THE CAMERA. SOME SPECIAL EFFECTS COMPANIES ARE EXPERTS IN ALL TYPES OF EFFECTS, WHILE SOME SPECIALIZE IN ONE PARTICULAR TYPE.

Based on the script and the director's vision, *Sasha Versus Zombies* won't need animatronics, miniatures, or car chases, and because the story takes place in Southern California, the crew doesn't need to worry about creating weather effects like fog, snow, or rain. But as the crew prepares to film the final showdown at Sasha's high school, the director calls in her SFX coordinator for a shot where some special effects are needed.

When Sasha and her friends finally arrive—tired, covered in gore, but still alive—at the high school, the director wants a surprise fight with a chopped-in-half zombie that crawls around on the ground in front of the high school entrance. After such a long trek to get to the high school, Sasha and her friends are not in the mood to deal with more zombie nonsense, and they give it the smackdown. The director decides she wants a simultaneous smackdown, where all four teens smush the zombie at once, causing a big geyser of blood to splash across the main doors of the high school. Which means it is time to call in the blood cannon!

The special effects supervisor and her team of technicians set up a blood cannon—a PVC pipe full of fake blood attached to an air compressor—and aim it at the doors. With the cameras pointed at the entrance and the cannon and the SFX crew carefully positioned out of frame, as soon as "Action!" is called, the SFX technician hits the trigger on the air compressor, and SPLAT! a stream of gore shoots across the doors. After a moment, the director yells, "CUT!" and the shot is captured.

After that shot, the director decides she also wants some shots of smoke drifting over the top of the high school and across the grounds to signal to the audience that things are not going well in Sasha's town. So, the special effects supervisor sets up some smokers, either handheld or on long poles, to create the effect.

Seeing the smoke gives the SFX supervisor an idea. What if Sasha and her friends trapped a group of zombies in one of the empty school buildings and . . . blew it up? That scene isn't in the script, but it's definitely something the crew could do. On the one hand, a scene like this would add a lot more to the budget and would be extremely complicated and tricky. On the other hand . . . it's a cool explosion. What do you want to do? Do you want to take the risk for an extra-dazzling scene?

A. Absolutely. Bring on the explosion!

Continue to the next page.

B. No way, it's not worth the risk.

Let's finish up the shoot.

Flip to page 83.

FIRESTARTER

F IRE IS COOL, BUT IT'S DANGEROUS EVEN WHEN IT'S BEING HANDLED by professionals. You can't have fire or explosions for a film shoot without hiring a *pyrotechnician*, a person who is trained in the storage, handling, and use of *pyrotechnics*, which are any fire-related special effects. This category includes fireworks, explosions, fires, flashes, and bombs.

Because the safety of so many people depends on the pyrotechnician, it's of the highest importance that she is properly trained, licensed, and certified. She works with the special effects team and the director to plan any pyrotechnics and is responsible for keeping everyone safe. A good pyrotechnician can create a dazzling pyro effect but also must be able to control and extinguish it quickly after the shot is captured. The cast and crew will also be exposed to any smoke and fumes created by pyrotechnics, so it's also important that the pyrotechnician uses the correct materials and chemicals that are nontoxic and environmentally friendly.

> A PYROTECHNICIAN IS THE PERSON WHO CREATES AND SAFELY SETS OFF THE FIREWORKS DISPLAY DURING CELEBRATIONS LIKE THE FOURTH OF JULY!

A pyrotechnician utilizes some very interesting tools in her trade. Balloons, Tupperware containers, and cardboard tubes are all surprisingly useful for pyrotechnics on a film. She also has to think outside of the box when doing her job. Maybe instead of blowing up a real car or a real building, a pyrotechnician might work with miniatures artists to create a small version to set on fire instead.

Besides the years of experience, it is crucial for a pyrotechnician to be precise and be cool and collected. Staying calm in the face of an intense explosion or blazing fire is a must!

Alright—ready for an explosion?

The pyrotechnician for *Sasha Versus Zombies* discusses the scene with the director and the special effects crew before getting started. Does the director want more flames or more smoke? Does she want a loud boom to go along with the explosion? How does she plan on capturing this explosion on camera? Will there be any stunt performers or actors in the shot? These are all questions that the pyrotechnician must ask and be thinking about while she plans and prepares. The worst thing that could happen would be someone getting injured during the shoot.

. . . The second-worst thing that could happen is to have the film's accountant and producer show up together right before the pyrotechnician sets her explosive charges off.

A. Uh-oh.

Continue to the next page.

GET OUT

●▼▼▼●▼●▼●▼▼●▼▼●▼▼●▼▼●●▼▼●▼●▼●▼●▼●▼▼▼▼●

IF THE PRODUCER *AND* THE PRODUCTION ACCOUNTANT BOTH GET THAT look—you know the one—on their faces, you know something is wrong.

It turns out that adding a huge explosion scene at the last minute not only adds too many extra costs to the production budget—plus, the extra insurance the producer would have to get in case of a fiery accident—but it is also going to put shooting behind schedule. Even though it would be a really cool effect, *Sasha Versus Zombies* would go over budget and over schedule, which means there wouldn't be enough money for post-production and enough time to shoot the rest of the movie.

Maybe on your next movie.

A. **Flip back to page 78.**

ACTORS
(ZOMBIES)

BOOM

ACTOR
(SASHA)

PA

CRAFT AND
CRAFT SERVICES

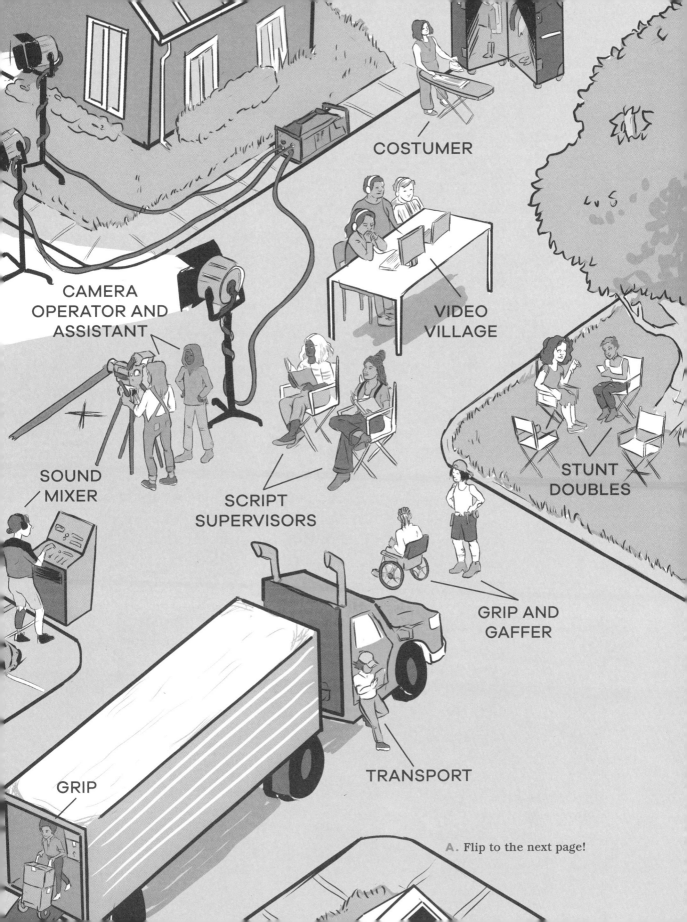

COSTUMER

CAMERA OPERATOR AND ASSISTANT

VIDEO VILLAGE

STUNT DOUBLES

SOUND MIXER

SCRIPT SUPERVISORS

GRIP AND GAFFER

GRIP

TRANSPORT

A. Flip to the next page!

DAY
ONE HUNDRED
AND EIGHTY

I WAS A TEENAGE ZOMBIE KILLER

YOU DID IT! YOU SHOT A MOVIE!

It's time to grab one last snack from crafty, remove the makeup from the actors, strike the lights and cameras—and return them if they were rented—and cords, put the costumes away, load all the gear into the grip and electric trucks, clean everything up, and head home. When production is over, wherever you shot the movie—whether it was in a warehouse on a studio lot or on location—should look exactly like it did before production began.

> MANY PLACES WHERE MOVIES HAVE BEEN SHOT LOOK TOTALLY NORMAL ONCE FILMING IS FINISHED! THE HOUSE WHERE NANCY FOUGHT FREDDY KRUEGER IN NIGHTMARE ON ELM STREET LOOKS LIKE A REGULAR HOME IN SOUTHERN CALIFORNIA.

The heads of each department are responsible for making sure their crew cleans up and properly returns or puts away all the equipment they used. Each of them will report to the producer.

After production *wraps*, which is just a fancy term for "finishes," many producers will throw a big *wrap party* for all the cast and crew. Big movies with huge budgets will often include custom wrap gifts for everyone, such as blankets or jackets embroidered with the name of the movie.

Although production is now finished, there is still more work to be done on the movie itself and still one final stage to go before you've got a completed film.

A. Flip to the next page on post-production.

POST-PRODUCTION

Although it seems like all the exciting stuff happens in production, post-production—or just post for short—is when a movie really comes to life. This is the stage when all the audio and visual elements of a movie are edited: the scenes are put together in the correct order, music and sound effects are added, and computer-generated special effects are created. If development is writing out a recipe, then pre-production is assembling the ingredients, production is mixing them together in the pan, and post-production is sticking the pan in the oven.

The director and producer will wave goodbye to their pre-production and production crews and say hello to a whole new crew of folks who will help them get this movie finished, or as they say in the film-making world, *in the can*.

28 DAYS LATER

MUCH NEEDS TO GET DONE DURING POST-PRODUCTION, AND ONE of a producer's first orders of business is to find someone to help her keep it all organized. A *post-production coordinator* is the woman who does just that.

In post-production, everyone works all at once. It's like an assembly line where each new element—from sound effects to CGI effects—is added along the way, in a particular order. The post-production coordinator works with all the people on the post-production team so that everything flows smoothly from one step to the next and the right people are communicating with each other. She also checks in to make sure that everyone is hitting their deadlines and not causing any delays. For example, the people adding sound effects cannot begin work until the movie has been edited, so the post-production coordinator makes sure that the editors stay on schedule. If they don't, that means everyone else on the team will be thrown off their deadlines. It's a job that requires a lot of, well, coordinating.

The post-production coordinator is the person who bridges the post-production team and the producer, communicating with both sides and guiding the post-production work so that it fits with the director's overall vision.

On films with large budgets and huge post-production teams, a producer will also hire a *post-production supervisor*. She helps hire people and works with the production accountant to make sure that the film isn't going over budget during the last stage of the filmmaking process. Remember, just like pre-production and post-production, if you spend too much money or take too long, the movie might not get made!

It's a lot to keep straight, but at the same time, it's a lot of fun being involved in so many different parts of the film at once. There are so many elements that must be added to a movie to finish it, and post-production coordinators help put it all together!

With a post-production coordinator secured to help you keep everything organized, it is time to dive into post-production on *Sasha Versus Zombies*!

A. Continue to the next page.

ONE CUT OF THE DEAD

A FTER PRODUCTION WRAPS, A DIRECTOR IS LEFT WITH HUNDREDS— sometimes thousands!—of hours of *raw footage*, which is the footage as it is captured on set with no changes or edits at all. To turn all those hours of raw footage into a polished, finished movie, you need the person who is arguably the most crucial part of the post-production process: the *editor*.

Editing is the process of taking footage and turning it into a movie, and it sometimes feels like editors spin straw into cinematic gold. Everything shot during production needs to be arranged in an order that tells the story; otherwise, it's just a random collection of scenes.

> THE EDITOR IS SOMETIMES KNOWN AS THE PICTURE EDITOR
> SO THAT NO ONE GETS CONFUSED WITH ALL THE OTHER TYPES
> OF EDITORS IN POST-PRODUCTION.

An editor watches all the footage, picks out all the best takes for each scene, then organizes them to tell the story the best. How does she do that? A lot of knowledge about timing and rhythm. She puts the shots together in a way that gives audiences the best experience and matches what the director wants the audience to feel while watching—fear during a horror movie, butterflies during a romantic movie, or awe during a science fiction movie. A *cut* is a technique used by editors to transition between scenes. Remember that jump scare in the beginning of *The Ring* where the screen suddenly shows the creepy girl in the closet? It's so scary because the editor used a *jump cut*, an abrupt transition between the shot of the main characters talking and the shot of the girl in the closet.

Part of the magic of editing is that there is no single or right way to do it. Editors use their knowledge of the story and the emotions they and the director want the audience to feel in combination with their own sense of rhythm, pace, and continuity to create the movie.

EDITOR KATE HACKETT, WHO WORKED ON HALF THE PICTURE, A DOCUMENTARY ABOUT WOMEN IN FILM, AND ON THE NETFLIX SERIES CHEER, WANTED TO BE AN EDITOR EVER SINCE SHE WAS A KID. SHE SAYS, "WHEN I WAS ABOUT TEN, I SAW JEAN COCTEAU'S BEAUTY AND THE BEAST. MY PARENTS HAD THE VIDEOTAPE BECAUSE THEY LOVED OLD FILMS AND FOREIGN FILMS. . . . [I]T HAD A LOT OF EDITING TRICKS IN IT. BEAUTY CHANGES FROM A SIMPLE DRESS TO A BEAUTIFUL JEWELED DRESS BY EDITING FROM ONE SIDE OF THE DOOR—IT'S JUST A SIMPLE CUT. SHE'S IN A BEAUTIFUL DRESS ON THE OTHER SIDE OF THE DOOR. AS A KID, I WOULD WATCH IT OVER AND OVER BECAUSE IT WAS SO MAGICAL."

Editors work in an area known as an *edit bay*—it is also known as an *edit suite*—which is a really fancy name for a windowless room with a computer equipped with a program designed for editing movies, a television to watch the movie on, plus some chairs and couches. Sometimes editors work alone, but often they work very closely with the director and the producer to discuss, revise, and try out new versions of scenes, so there can be a lot of collaboration involved. Editing a movie usually takes months, so the editor and director get to know each other very well after spending so much time in the edit bay together!

SOMETIMES, A PRODUCER AND A DIRECTOR WILL DISAGREE ON HOW THE MOVIE SHOULD BE EDITED. OFTEN, THE PRODUCER GETS FINAL CUT, WHICH MEANS FINAL SAY ON THE FILM EDIT. A DIRECTOR'S CUT OF A MOVIE IS A DIRECTOR'S PREFERRED VERSION OF A MOVIE.

It's essential for an editor to be patient because she needs to watch a scene again and again, tinkering with the timing and cuts until they're just right. Editors might end up cutting a scene a few different ways to see what works best.

So, how do people learn how to be editors? Some editors go to college for filmmaking, and others are self-taught. It is also common for editors to start out working on short films to get experience and then work their way up to feature films. It is easy to start experimenting with editing, and the best way to become an editor is to practice doing it yourself! If you have a smartphone or a computer to work on, you've got all the tools you need. To help you to strengthen your skills, you can also try directing to learn how shots do and don't go together. You can go out and shoot a short video on a camera or smartphone, then upload the video into a video editor and play around with how shots fit together. Just keep practicing!

There are several stages to the editing process, and *logging* is the first. This is when the director and editor for *Sasha Versus Zombies* watch the collected dailies from the entire shoot, after which the editor sorts them, keeping an eye out for great moments of zombie action and cool shots.

After the dailies have been watched and sorted roughly in the order that they happen in the story, the editor can move on to the next stage, which is creating the *first assembly cut.* With all the scenes in roughly the right sequence, she can play around and see which shots best convey the scene. Maybe the best way to show the zombies overtaking Sasha's house is to cut to a shot of one of Sasha's friends looking out the window with a terrified expression. Or would it be scarier to start with a shot of the front door shaking from the force of the zombies banging on it? Having a lot of options for the editor to choose from during the editing process is why directors like to shoot a scene from different angles and distances. With countless ways to arrange each scene, every choice gives her the opportunity to tell the story slightly differently. Editors aren't afraid to experiment!

Putting the first assembly cut together usually takes a few weeks, and when it is finished *Sasha Versus Zombies* is ready for the next stage, called the *rough cut*. This is when the order of the scenes is finalized and checked for continuity, and it is a process that can take months. This is also the best stage for the director to make big changes to the cut. Perhaps she watches the first assembly cut and decides that she wants the film to be a little scarier—she wants to really show off those zombies! She also wants to focus a little more on Sasha and her friends. With these directions in mind, the editor starts cutting *Sasha Versus Zombies* so that it includes more shots of Sasha and her friends' reactions, so the audience feels more connected to these characters by seeing more of how they are emotionally affected by the hordes of undead taking over their small town. To up the scare factor, the editor finds takes where the actors look extra terrified and makes abrupt cuts in the scenes, so the zombies seem to pop out of nowhere.

Once the editor, director, and producer approve the rough cut of the movie from start to finish, this rough cut is now called the *first cut*. At this point, the sequence of scenes in *Sasha Versus Zombies* is basically set. The movie might still look and sound unfinished, because sound and other effects are added after this stage, but the length and the order of the scenes is close to the final version.

Finally, the editor refines *Sasha Versus Zombies* by working out all the details and making sure every scene and shot is perfect, which transforms the first cut into a *fine cut*. For example, the editor watches one of the scenes where Sasha is hiding from zombies in her house and realizes that she can remove a few seconds of Sasha catching her breath. This quickens the pace of the scene and makes the moment when a zombie breaks the living room window extra scary!

After a few more weeks of fine tuning on the movie, the director and the producer join the editor in the edit suite to watch the new fine cut. Everyone loves it, and it is now the *final cut* of *Sasha Versus Zombies*, ready for the rest of the post-production team to add sound, music, and visual effects.

A. Did you choose practical zombies?

Flip to the next page.

B. Did you choose CGI zombies?

Flip to page 99.

AN UNQUIET PLACE

IT'S TOUGH TO BELIEVE, BUT BEFORE THE MID-1920S, FILMS WERE totally silent. Today, sound is a crucial part of the experience of a movie. You might think of movies as a visual medium, but in the modern world, they are so much more. What would films be without the roar of dinosaurs in *Jurassic Park*, "The Imperial March" when Darth Vader comes on screen in *Star Wars*, or Angela Lansbury singing "A Tale as Old as Time" in *Beauty and the Beast*?

> SOUND AND MUSIC IN MOVIES ARE SORTED INTO TWO CATEGORIES. DIEGETIC SOUND IS ANY SOUND HAPPENING IN THE WORLD OF THE FILM OR THAT A CHARACTER IN THE MOVIE COULD HEAR. DIALOGUE, A SONG PLAYING OUT OF A CHARACTER'S HEADPHONES, OR THE SOUND OF A CHAIR SCRAPING AS THAT CHARACTER GETS UP FROM THE KITCHEN TABLE ARE ALL EXAMPLES OF DIEGETIC SOUND. NON-DIEGETIC SOUND IS ANY SOUND THAT DOESN'T HAPPEN IN THE WORLD OF THE FILM, SUCH AS VOICE-OVER NARRATION OR A THEME SONG.

Post-production sound work is a world of musical compositions, pop songs, sound effects, and dialogue. Just like other film departments, the sound department is a team of talented people creating amazing stuff. The woman who hires and manages everyone is the *supervising sound editor* or *sound supervisor*. She keeps her team organized as the audio for the film is created, edited, and processed, plus she works with the post-production coordinator to keep everyone on schedule. Making sure all the audio is created, edited, and processed is her responsibility. For a feature film, there's a lot of audio that her team will have to create and work with!

The first member of the sound supervisor's team is the *dialogue editor*. She is tasked with making sure all the dialogue is clean, as in, not fuzzy or hard to hear. It's her job to take the dialogue captured by the production sound mixer and the boom operator and adjust all the levels on it so that everything is clear and audible. If one actor has a louder voice than the other actors in a scene, the dialogue editor will adjust so the audience can hear everyone equally. While watching the final cut from the picture editor, the dialogue editor will make sure the words line up with the mouth movements of the actors. A movie would look really silly without her work! She also has the fun job of modulating, or changing the tone, pitch, and strength, of an actor's voice if it is, for example, coming out of a speaker, walkie talkie, or some other device that would change how their voice sounds.

While going through the dialogue, if the dialogue editor finds any lines that aren't clean or need to be rerecorded, then the sound supervisor hires an *ADR mixer*. ADR stands for *automated dialogue replacement*. There are a bunch of reasons that dialogue might need to get replaced. Maybe the actor flubbed the line a little bit and no one noticed. Maybe background noise made the line tough to hear. Maybe the director, after watching the finished final cut from the picture editor, decided to change a line.

The dialogue editor will send the ADR mixer a list of lines that need to be recorded, and the ADR mixer will set up a recording booth with microphones and call in the actors (or, if they aren't available, actors who sound like them) to record new lines. This is sometimes called *dubbing* or *looping*. While the actor is recording, the ADR mixer gives them cues and sometimes even reads the lines of other actors in the scene or shows the scene on a screen in the booth for them. If the actor is rerecording lines instead of recording new ones, the ADR mixer will watch the recording closely to match the mouth movements in the video recording of the scene. Finally, the ADR mixer will pass the recordings to an *ADR editor* to edit the new lines into the film. You can see why it is so important to have a good post-production coordinator and sound supervisor to keep everyone communicating! With bigger movies come more sounds, so sometimes the sound supervisor will hire some *sound assistants* to help out.

All these post-production sound jobs require a solid grasp of acoustics and knowledge of recording and sound equipment. If you are interested in recording, this might be a great job for you! It helps if you've got sharp hearing and good timing, too. There is no one way to get into cinematic sound work. Some people go to college for filmmaking, some go to college for music, and some don't go to college at all but rather teach themselves or get mentored by an established professional. There are lots of online classes in sound work you can check out if you are looking for a way to learn more.

⁂

If the production sound mixer and boom operator did a great job during the shooting of *Sasha Versus Zombies*, there wouldn't be too much to do in ADR. However, after watching the final cut of the movie, the director might decide that she wants to have more *exertions*, which are the sounds actors make in a scene when they are exerting themselves. That could mean falling, exercising, or in the case of this movie, fighting. A fight scene isn't quite the same without a bunch of OOFs and YAHs!

So, the post-production coordinator works with the sound supervisor and ADR mixer to schedule a time for the actors playing Sasha and her friends, and even some of the zombie actors, to come into the recording booth—though not all at the same time—and record some exertions. Many actors have an easier time recording them when they are physically moving around and swinging their limbs. All the actors have a fun time yelling AH and OH and OOMPH, and the zombie actors have even more fun growling out sounds of the undead.

All these human and zombie sounds are great; however, *Sasha Versus Zombies* still needs some *sound effects*. For those, we've got to meet the *foley artist*.

A. Flip to page 102.

DAY TWO HUNDRED AND FIFTY

EFFECTS FROM ANOTHER WORLD

THE RISE OF DIGITAL TECHNOLOGY DIDN'T SIMPLY CHANGE HOW movies were shot; it also changed what was seen on screen. *Visual effects*, or *VFX*, are different from practical effects because they're created by a computer after filming instead of on camera during filming. But that doesn't make them any less cool! Visual effects are the manipulation or creation of any imagery for the screen that does not exist in real life, including any creatures, environments, people, or stunts—that are either imaginary or would be impractical or too dangerous for a human to do in real life. Often, VFX are integrated with live action, such as Pepper Potts's suit in the Avengers movies. Gwyneth Paltrow is wearing the costume in real life, but parts of the suit—the parts that move—are computer generated and therefore are virtual effects.

The woman leading this team is the *VFX supervisor*, and all the VFX created and all the *VFX artists* who make this movie magic are her responsibility. Just like the other department heads do, she works closely with the director and acts as the communication point between her VFX team and the rest of the post-production department.

> BECAUSE VFX ARE OFTEN USED WITH REAL-LIFE ACTORS, ON SOME MOVIES THE VFX TEAM GETS INVOLVED IN PRE-PRODUCTION OR PRODUCTION TO MAKE SURE THAT THE SHOTS CAPTURED BY THE DP WILL WORK WELL WITH CGI IMAGERY. THE TEAM MIGHT EVEN MAKE SOME CGI ART AHEAD OF TIME TO SHOW THE DIRECTOR WHAT THEY PLAN ON MAKING.

VFX artists typically create three types of digital imagery for movies:

- *CGI* or *computer generated imagery*: These are digitally created graphics, usually 3D ones. This could be a massive, fire-breathing dragon, a dancing mouse in a top hat, or even something a little more everyday, like filling in a field with a marching digital army. In fact, the Lord of the Rings films used this to create colossal armies of orcs!

- *Compositing*: This is where, with the use of green screens, artists are able to take different objects, people, or backgrounds and combine them to look like they're all in the same place. Although computers are used to achieve this effect now, compositing has been around for a long time. Early films in the twentieth century placed huge paintings—called *matte paintings* because they had to be matte so that light didn't reflect off them—of landscapes, cities, or other sets behind the scene and filmed them in such a way that it looked like the actors were really in that location. A great example of this is the shots in *Wizard of Oz* of the Emerald City!

- *Motion capture*, or *mo-cap*: This is a technique that combines real-life movement with digital imagery. Mo-cap involves digitally recording an actor's movements and then pasting them onto a 3D digital model. To do this, the actor wears a mo-cap suit, which is a tight, black, full-body suit covered in special markers that the camera can track and record. The VFX team can even cover the actor's face in dot stickers so that the camera can track and record her facial expressions. If a mo-cap includes the actor's facial expressions, it is called a *performance capture*. For example, Zoe Saldana used performance capture for her role in *Avatar*!

VFX artists have an eye for photography, light, and composition and are great at collaboration and teamwork. Many films have lots of VFX artists working at the same time to create visual effects, all reporting to a VFX supervisor who tracks everyone's progress on their work, so it's essential for the VFX artists to be great at working together. Besides being talented with art, good VFX artists are skilled with computers and the various VFX programs, such as Adobe After Effects, ZBrush, and Unreal Engine.

THE FIRST-EVER WOMAN TO WIN AN OSCAR FOR VISUAL EFFECTS WAS SUZANNE M. BENSON, WHO WON IN 1987 FOR HER WORK ON THE FILM ALIENS!

During pre-production, you chose to have CGI zombies, so now it's time to make them!

When the director is planning the look of the zombies during the early stages of the filmmaking process, she might have a meeting with the VFX supervisor where they decide to have a mix of CGI zombies and mo-cap zombies. While the VFX team gets started on creating some digital zombies to put into the scenes, the director heads on over to the mo-cap studio.

AN EARLY FORM OF MOTION CAPTURE WAS CALLED ROTOSCOPING, WHICH INVOLVED TRACING FOOTAGE OF A REAL ACTOR MOVING AND ANIMATING IT. THE FIRST USE OF ROTOSCOPING IN A FILM WAS IN 1937'S SNOW WHITE AND THE SEVEN DWARFS!

In the studio, the director works with the motion capture actors to get fantastically creepy zombie performances. These are added to the live-action footage, along with the other CGI zombies the VFX artists created. Now the director has zombies that have a lot of movement and emotion from the mo-cap actors as well as zombies perfect for hordes and for background using CGI.

But is a zombie still a zombie without scary sounds? Now that *Sasha Versus Zombies* has lots of great-looking zombies, it's time to make them moan, groan, and snarl.

A. Flip to the next page.

ISLAND OF LOST SOUNDS

MANY PARTS OF THE MOVIE EXPERIENCE ARE LARGER THAN LIFE, so you might not realize that the sounds you hear are among them.

From the fantastical, such as the buzzing of a lightsaber, to the everyday, such as a door shutting, sounds in film are carefully thought out and crafted. In your everyday life, you might not notice many of the sounds that surround you like fabric swishing or feet tapping, but they're extremely important to an immersive movie experience. They're called *foley*, and the woman tasked with creating all those sounds is a *foley artist*.

A foley artist creates and recreates sounds in post-production to enhance their quality. The production sound crew's main goal is to capture the dialogue, so some of the other sounds that are important to the scene might not be as audible. It is up to the foley artist to make sure the audience can hear sounds like slamming doors, cracking knuckles, swirling capes, breaking bones, smashing windows, tapping feet, and groaning ropes, just to name a few. The way she achieves this is with the use of props.

For example, let's look at footsteps. This is a fairly straightforward sound to make, so in her shop, the foley artist sets up whatever flooring the character in the film is walking on, places microphones nearby, and then walks on the flooring in the same type of shoes the character is wearing. To make sure the sounds are in sync with the actor's actions, the foley artist plays a cut of the movie in her shop to make sure the sounds match the movements on screen. Basically, these are the main tools of her trade—props, a viewing screen, and sensitive microphones.

There are three types of sounds that foley artists need to make: footsteps, which are self-explanatory; movement, such as arms swishing around in a raincoat; and props, such as a bucket dropping.

Then there are times that foley artists are asked to create sounds that do not exist in real life, which means they have to do a whole lot of experimenting to figure out the right sound—they're called foley *artists* for a reason! For example, Godzilla's roar was originally created by rubbing a double bass with a glove covered in pine resin, while the growls of a Jack Russell terrier were used to create the roar of the T. rex in *Jurassic*

Park, and the slithering noise of the T-1000 sliding between metal bars in *Terminator 2* was created by recording the sound of dog food being sucked out of the can. Gross . . . but still pretty cool!

> THE CREEPY SOUNDS OF THE 2020 REMAKE OF THE INVISIBLE MAN WERE.
> CREATED BY EMMY AWARD—WINNING FOLEY ARTIST JOANNA FANG!

If you're interested in becoming a foley artist, you should try recreating and recording sounds at home with a smartphone, computer, or any other recording device. See what sort of sounds you can invent!

Speaking of unpleasant sounds, the foley artist working on *Sasha Versus Zombies* has to create some pretty gross zombie sounds. Although they look disgusting on screen, you might be surprised to learn that most gore sound effects are created with fruits and vegetables. Snapping celery is used for breaking bones, for example. In fact, the sounds in one of the most iconic stabby scenes of all time, the infamous shower scene in Alfred Hitchcock's *Psycho*, were created by stabbing a bunch of melons. You could find the sounds of a zombie fight right at the farmer's market!

For this film, the foley artist needs a bushel of produce to make the sounds of the zombies' snapping bones, bashed heads, and squished guts. Before she gets to work though, first she's spent a few weeks watching a cut of the movie and talking to the director about what sort of sounds are needed. Then, she gets to smashing, smushing, and squishing!

She also makes the footsteps of Sasha and her friends running down the streets, the slammed doors as they try to keep the zombies out of Sasha's house, the slide of nylon string as Sasha laces up her Doc Martens, and the metal TWANG! as one of Sasha's friends leans against a locker to rest when they finally reach the high school. No horror film—well, no film at all, really—is the same without a foley artist's magic.

Now, the sound of squished brains might be music to a zombie's ears—if they still have ears—but what about actual music?

There are two types of music used in film. One is a *score*, which is a piece of instrumental music composed specifically for the movie performed by a live orchestra for recording. The other is a *soundtrack*, which are songs chosen and licensed, and sometimes even recorded specifically for the film. Hiring someone to compose, perform, and record a film score definitely takes a while and can be extremely expensive— remember that you've got to hire a whole orchestra! On the one hand, with the right composer, her phenomenal score might be just what your movie needs to feel epic. On the other hand, creating a great soundtrack is quicker and, depending on which songs you choose, can be far less expensive and equally amazing. Which one do you think would be a better choice for *Sasha Versus Zombies*?

A. **You want a cool soundtrack.**

   Continue to the next page.

B. **You want an epic score.**

   Flip to page 108.

30 SONGS OF NIGHT

A N INCREDIBLE SOUNDTRACK CAN MAKE YOUR MOVIE ICONIC. EVEN if you've never seen the films, you picture the end of *The Breakfast Club* when you hear "Don't You Forget About Me," or Dolly Parton in *9 to 5* when you hear "9 to 5," or Jack and Rose on the bow of the Titanic when you hear "My Heart Will Go On."

Music is what sets the emotional tone for a movie. No matter what is being shown on screen, the audience can tell what emotion the director wants them to feel by the music that is playing.

The woman who chooses the songs is the *music supervisor*. She's the head of the music department, and she works with the director to decide which songs will help convey the emotion she wants the viewer to experience when they're watching the movie. During their meetings, the director shares her ideas and the music supervisor will suggest songs, but often, directors already know which songs they want to use for certain scenes. Sometimes, they decide to record an original song for the movie.

Once the two of them have settled on which songs they want, the music supervisor works with the producer to make sure they can afford to *license* them. When a music supervisor pays for permission to use a song in a film, that's called licensing. If a song by the original artist is too expensive, one compromise is to get permission and pay the artist to be allowed to have another musician cover the original song for the movie. If even getting permission to cover the song is too expensive, the music supervisor will search for a good substitute. Every filmmaker would love a song from someone like Beyoncé or Janelle Monáe in their movie, but most of the time, they've got to find a less expensive alternative!

WHITNEY HOUSTON'S FAMOUS SONG "I WILL ALWAYS LOVE YOU" WAS RECORDED FOR THE FILM THE BODYGUARD. IT WAS A COVER OF DOLLY PARTON'S ORIGINAL SONG!

Once the music supervisor has permission to use the songs, then she watches the film with the director and finds the perfect moment to play them. Traditionally, songs are played at either the beginning of a movie or as the end credits roll, but sometimes, there's an excellent scene during the film to place the song. Can you imagine *Guardians of the Galaxy* without "Come and Get Your Love"?

Music supervisors have an incredibly wide knowledge of music. A great music supervisor can think of several songs—or substitutes—from all different time periods, styles, and genres. She also has an incredibly wide knowledge of music licensing and the people skills to negotiate with the folks who own the rights to the songs she wants! If you've got an encyclopedic knowledge of songs and love movies, this might be the perfect job for you! Can you think of examples of great uses of songs in movies?

* llllllll*

For *Sasha Versus Zombies*, the director wants to use several songs during the movie, but the most important one is, of course, for the final showdown at the high school. During this scene, Sasha figures out that the best way to destroy all the zombies is to have her friends lure them all out onto the football field with the cafeteria's leftover meatloaf and then run them all down—the zombies, not her friends!—with the groundskeeper's gigantic lawnmower.

But what song would be best to use? Something that would be sure to get some laughs would be to pair a bunch of squished zombies with a song that is upbeat like "Good as Hell" by Lizzo and Ariana Grande, or "Don't Stop Believin'" by Journey. Or the director might want something that feels heavier, like "Thunderstruck" by AC/DC or "Don't Fear the Reaper" by Blue Oyster Cult. Maybe something really epic like "Heroes" by David Bowie is the way to go. After talking, the music supervisor and director decide to go with something that is a little funny, heavy, *and* epic with an all-female hard rock cover of "Dead Man's Party" by Oingo Boingo. And, of course, the music supervisor will save the producer money by licensing a cover instead of the original version.

Then she hires the right band to record the song. Once the band finishes recording the song, all she has to do is watch a cut of *Sasha Versus Zombies* with the director to figure out the exact right spot to put the song. Should it start as soon as we see shots of Sasha's friends luring the zombies with trays of old meatloaf? Or as we hear the lawnmower starting up? Or the second the scene of Sasha riding the lawnmower onto the field begins? Timing is key with music in films, and the music supervisor needs to make sure that she gets the maximum emotional impact from a song.

The music supervisor and director decide to start the song as Sasha's friends begin to lure the zombies out onto the field. They time it perfectly so that just as the first frame of Sasha on the lawnmower is on screen, the chorus begins—about a party where no one's alive!

Okay, so we've got our ADR, dialogue, sound effects, and some killer—pun intended—music. But we're not finished with sound yet. Now it's time to learn about *ambient sound*, which is just as cool as it—yes, another pun—sounds.

A. Flip to page 112.

SOUND-SPIRIA

MUSIC IS ONE OF THE MOST IMPORTANT, BUT UNSEEN—LITERALLY!— parts of a film. You might not realize it while you're watching, but the emotions you feel are often being guided by a movie's *score*, the instrumental music written for a film. In the early days of the movie industry and silent films, movie screenings were accompanied by live bands or orchestras who played music for the audience.

When movies finally could add sounds and dialogue, the job of *film composer* was born so that movies could have music, too. She is the one who writes the big swell of romantic music when two characters finally kiss; the slow, sad piece when a character passes away; or the terrifying screech of strings as a character goes into the basement to investigate a weird noise—no matter how loudly you yell for them not to!

> THE FIRST WOMAN TO WIN AN OSCAR FOR BEST ORIGINAL SCORE WAS HILDUR GUDNADOTTIR FOR THE FILM JOKER IN 2020.

Like the rest of the post-production team, the composer works closely with the director to decide exactly which scenes in the movie should have a score, because not all scenes need music behind them—sometimes silence works even better. The general rule is that about half of the scenes in a movie need to have a score behind them. Then, after the director and the composer decide on the scenes to be scored, the composer begins experimenting to see what sort of music she should write to accompany them.

To get started, she writes and records multiple versions of a *theme*, which is basically the melodic subject of a musical piece that can be repeated. Then the composer can write variations on that theme, in a higher or lower tempo, for example, depending on what is happening with the character or the story line. For example, if the character has a death scene, the composer could record a slower, sadder version of their theme to play during the moment. The Star Wars films make great use of themes—many of the main characters, such as Princess Leia and Darth Vader, have their own specific music that plays while they are on screen.

Once the director approves of the themes and additional pieces of music the composer has created—sometimes she has to write and record many different versions until the director likes it!—then she gets to work hiring the musicians and staff to record the music she wrote. Some composers hire a whole orchestra to record their music, and others create the entire score for the film on their own, using instruments or computer programs. With the rise of digital music technology, some composers use only computers and don't need to read sheet music at all.

After the score is recorded, the composer usually works with a *music editor*, who is responsible for editing the recording of the score and syncing it to the film. She makes sure everything is timed perfectly, so that each musical moment is matched up exactly with its corresponding moment in the film. Remember how the music swells the second after Captain America says, "Avengers . . . assemble" in *Avengers: Endgame*? That moment was created by a music editor syncing the score up correctly!

OFTEN, THE MUSIC EDITOR WILL MAKE A TEMPORARY SCORE, CALLED A "TEMP SCORE" FOR SHORT, TO PUT TO THE FILM TO GIVE THE DIRECTOR AN IDEA OF WHAT THE COMPOSER HAS IN MIND. SHE MIGHT GRAB PIECES OF SCORES FROM OTHER MOVIES TO CREATE THE TEMP SCORE. FOR EXAMPLE, SHE COULD TAKE A REALLY SCARY SCORE, LET'S SAY THE BAH-DUM, BAH-DUM PART OF JAWS WHEN THE SHARK IS STALKING THE BOAT, AND PUT IT TO A SCARY SCENE IN THE ROUGH CUT OF THE MOVIE TO SHOW THE DIRECTOR THAT THE COMPOSER WANTS TO DO SOMETHING SIMILARLY SCARY FOR THAT SCENE.

Most film composers start out in a college program for music, but just like many other people who work in film, some are self-taught and get practice working on short films made by friends. You could practice scoring a film by writing a piece of music and syncing it up with a scene from a movie that already exists. All you need is a computer and some music software—there are free programs online you can use!

THE FILM COMPOSER ANGELA MORLEY BECAME THE FIRST OPENLY TRANSGENDER PERSON TO BE NOMINATED FOR AN OSCAR IN 1974 FOR HER SCORE FOR THE LITTLE PRINCE.

A score can very quickly convey to an audience the exact genre of a movie. And since *Sasha Versus Zombies* is a horror movie, a creepy score would help audiences know right away what they are watching. The wrong music can ruin a scene. If there was a silly piece of music with an accordion playing during a zombie fight scene, it would feel like something funny was going on, instead of something scary. Audiences might be confused and think Sasha was about to get a pie thrown in her face instead of a bunch of zombie gore.

To avoid that, the *Sasha Versus Zombies* composer wants to get an extra epic feel, so she decides to record the score with a live orchestra. She writes a score with big, sweeping strings for triumphant moments, intense kettle drums for the scary fight scenes, and an ominous theme with some high-pitched piano notes for the zombies.

Once the score is written and approved by the director, the composer then books some recording dates with an orchestra she hired. She is present for the recording to conduct the orchestra and make sure the music is being played as she wants it. As the musicians play the pieces of music, the corresponding scenes from *Sasha Versus Zombies* are shown on a big screen behind the orchestra. The composer watches the screen as everyone plays—the creepy piece when the zombies lurk in Sasha's front yard, the intense piece when the zombie horde isn't fooled by Sasha's zombie makeup, the sweeping piece when Sasha's friends lure them all onto the football field and Sasha runs them all down—the zombies, not her friends!—with the groundskeeper's gigantic lawnmower.

With the music finally recorded, the music editor syncs it up with the final cut. Boom—*Sasha Versus Zombies* is scored!

Okay, so we've got our ADR, dialogue, sound effects, and some killer—pun intended—music. But we're not finished with sound yet. Now it's time to learn about *ambient sound*, which is just as cool as it—yes, another pun—sounds.

A. Flip to page 112.

DAY
THREE HUNDRED
AND SIXTY-FIVE

WE ARE STILL HEAR

DIALOGUE, MUSIC, AND SOUND EFFECTS—OH MY! TO FINISH UP sound in post-production, there's one more type of sound to add to a film. *Ambient* sound is essentially any sound in the background of a movie, like the rumble of a train in the distance, the roaring of the ocean, or the wind in the trees. Any sound that contributes to the atmosphere of a scene is considered ambient. Of course, someone needs to either record or create these sounds, and that woman is the *sound designer*, who is sometimes called the *sound editor*. If you've ever been creeped out by the ambient sounds of an abandoned hospital in a horror movie or felt cozy listening to the ambient sounds of a magical creature's kitchen in a fantasy movie, that was the work of a sound designer. And they love weird noises!

Often for her work, the sound designer must create the sounds she needs, and she usually does this with the help of computer programs. Sometimes, she has to invent new sounds, like the sound designer did for *The Matrix* for the bullets whooshing past Neo as he dodges them. Other times, she has to manipulate existing ones like in *Selma*, where the sound designer worked with real sounds of people running down the street.

> MILDRED IATROU MORGAN AND AI-LING LEE WERE THE FIRST ALL-FEMALE TEAM NOMINATED FOR AN OSCAR FOR BEST SOUND FOR THEIR FILM, *LA LA LAND*, IN 2017. AI-LING LEE WAS THE FIRST ASIAN AMERICAN WOMAN NOMINATED FOR THAT CATEGORY!

When the sound designer finishes her work, the sound for the movie is complete. It's the last piece of the audible puzzle. Now there's ambient sound, dialogue, sound effects, and music, so it is time for someone to take all these separate sounds and combine them, like a noise Voltron. The woman responsible for pulling all these elements together into one aural environment is the *rerecording mixer* (sometimes called the *sound mixer*, not to be confused with the one in production). It is her job to create the movie's overall soundscape.

The sound mixer balances all the various sounds in a film—score, songs, sound effects, dialogue—and makes sure they are working in harmony. Because of her hard work, the audience can still clearly hear the dialogue when music is playing in the background, and the sound effects aren't being drowned out by the ambient noises. Just like the rest of the sound department, the sound designer and the sound mixer work closely with the director to make sure her vision—which seems like a weird word to use for sound!—is being realized and the post-production coordinator to make sure everything is being created and delivered on time.

You can experiment with sound design, editing, and mixing right at home! Record sounds, such as wind or subway noises, with a recorder or a smartphone and then upload the files to a computer. There are lots of free programs online to play around with those sounds and see what new sounds you can make!

The sound designer for *Sasha Versus Zombies* has to recreate the sounds of a suburban neighborhood—lawns being mowed, dogs barking, cars driving at reasonable speeds down the street. These are the sort of sounds you might not immediately notice when watching the film, but they would make the scenes feel more real. For the zombies, the sound designer would probably have to create a soundscape of shambling, dragging, and . . . chewing. Gross.

The sound mixer then adds all those sounds to the dialogue of Sasha and her friends, the ADR everyone recorded, the sound effects from the foley artist, and the music to form one big audio file that is perfectly balanced. Boom! The sound for *Sasha Versus Zombies* is in the can.

With all the sound finally complete, the movie is very close to the finish line. But it's not done yet! A movie never looks fully finished and polished without this next step.

A. Continue to the next page.

THE COLORIST FROM OUTER SPACE

EVEN AFTER SEVERAL ROUNDS OF EDITING, A FILM DOES NOT REACH its final visual form until it is *color corrected* and *color graded*. You know how, before you upload a photo to Instagram, you might add a filter to your selfie or adjust the brightness, shadows, or colors? When you do that, you are giving your cute selfie a little bit of color grading or color correction.

The woman who does it for a whole movie is known as the *colorist*. Her work is broken down into two categories: correcting and grading. Color correcting is when she fixes any mistakes that were made during shooting that would affect the color of a shot. Maybe a scene took so long to shoot that the sun moved and the lighting looks slightly different in each shot. Or maybe the camera crew used a red gel in some of the shots in the scene but forgot to put the gel on the lights for the other shots. Or maybe one scene just looks too bright and doesn't match the rest of the movie. All these problems can be fixed by the colorist.

In color grading, the colorist takes the footage and changes aspects like the brightness, saturation, contrast, or color temperature to help the shots all feel consistent and to emphasize certain colors to help tell the story. For example, in *Pan's Labyrinth*, all the scenes in the fantasy world have a warm, gold color, while all the scenes in the real world have more of a cool, blue hue. To decide on the color palette of the film, the colorist works with the director of photography and—you guessed it—the director to find just the right one. The colorist works in a room called the color suite, which is sort of like the edit suite that the editor works in. The color suite must have bright, neutral lighting so the colorist can properly assess the way the film looks. No lava lamps allowed in there! She works on a computer with a color program like Adobe Premiere Pro that is much, much fancier and more complicated than Instagram.

Colorists, as you might expect, have an incredible eye for detail and color, and an extensive knowledge of color theory. If you've ever tried to tell a story just with color, or love learning the meaning of color, or are interested in color theory, this would be a fun job for you!

Remember back in pre-production, when the DP and director decided that they wanted *Sasha Versus Zombies* to be bright but creepy? The colorist is the last person on the team to contribute to this color palette and bring the director's vision to life. Things like Sasha's green Doc Martens, the crimson zombie blood, and the pink accents in Sasha's bedroom all stand out more after the colorist does her pass on the film. She helps make all the work of the production designer, the DP, the costume designer, the hair and makeup artists, the prop master—everyone, really—truly pop. The colorist makes everyone else on the film team, from development to post-production, look good.

When she is done with her work on *Sasha Versus Zombies*, it looks and sounds like a finished film. However, it isn't *quite* a finished film yet. There's one final step to completing the movie, like putting the cherry on top of a sundae.

A. Continue to the next page to finish the movie!

CRAWL

WHEN A FILM IS FINISHED, IT IS TIME TO WRAP IT UP IN A BOW. Well, sort of. You can't show a film in a movie theater without the *credits*! So many incredibly talented and wonderful crew members helped you get here. Now you've got to make sure they get credit for all their hard work up on the screen by acknowledging their name and contributions.

Before a movie starts, you see the *opening credits*, which acknowledge the most important members of a film production and show the title of the movie. These will include the logo, many of which are animated in today's films, of the production company that made the movie. If multiple production companies help make—or just provide money to, known as *financing*—a movie, all their logos will appear. After the production companies is usually the *title sequence*, which shows the name of the movie. Nowadays, title sequences can be very elaborate, with moving type or animation. The woman who creates them is known as a *main title designer*. Her job is to create something interesting to the audience and reflective of the movie. For example, in the original *The Addams Family* movie, the opening credits flash in front of swirls of creepy mist that looks like the mist surrounding their infamous house. After the title sequence, *title cards* will play, which are full-screen images featuring text that credit the big stars of the film and major crew members. That's when you see DIRECTED BY: THAT LADY and STARRING: THAT OTHER LADY on one full-screen image.

Finally, when the movie is finished, the *closing credits* roll. These are called the *end crawl* because they crawl slowly up the screen. The end crawl credits every single person involved in the entire film production. In huge-budget movies, the end crawl can take ten whole minutes to watch! But those ten minutes are important, because everyone involved in a movie deserves that onscreen credit. As you know now, it is really hard work to make a movie.

There are companies dedicated to creating end crawls—Endcrawl.com being one of the most frequently used by filmmakers—who get a list of everyone involved in development, pre-production, production, and post-production from the producers. Using that list, they plug everyone's names into a template, though the producers might ask them to use a certain font or color to match the rest of the movie.

~~~~~~~~

Wow, so many incredible folks to put into the end crawl of *Sasha Versus Zombies*! You met all kinds of wonderful women. It would be so cool to see all their names up on the screen in a movie theater, or at home on the television. With your opening and ending credits created and edited into the final film, are you ready to finally finish this movie?

A. Oh my goodness. It's time!

    Continue to the next page!

SASHA THE ZOMBIE SLAYER

OH MY GOSH, YOU DID IT! YOU MADE A MOVIE! NOW YOU CAN GRAB some soda, a big bucket of popcorn, and some candy and see your hard work up on the big screen. It's time to bring *Sasha Versus Zombies* to the world, so other kids can see it and go on Sasha's journey with her.

At a film premiere, the cast and crew are invited to walk the red carpet and see the film up on a big movie theater screen. Film premieres are not for the public—they are usually scheduled right before a film is released. Along with the cast and crew, movie critics and people from the press are also invited to watch the movie—so hopefully they'll write a good review about it in a newspaper or magazine or on a movie website! If a film is being released internationally, sometimes there are multiple premieres, one in each country it comes out in. The biggest premieres, however, are usually in Hollywood, California.

HOLLYWOOD HAS BEEN USING A RED CARPET TO PREMIERE MOVIES SINCE THE 1920S! THE FIRST-EVER PREMIERE, FOR THE FILM ROBIN HOOD— NOT THE ANIMATED ONE!—WAS IN 1922. A RED CARPET WAS USED FOR THE GUESTS AND EVER SINCE, IT HAS BEEN ASSOCIATED WITH FILM PREMIERES.

The cool part about filmmaking is that each movie is like a fingerprint—infinitely variable. Some films are very big, with a huge budget and lots of cast and crew. Some are much smaller. Some films have all of the crew members you met in this book, some have more. Some have less! It is important to remember that each movie is special and has its own unique needs.

So, the next time you watch a movie, *really* watch it and think about all the things you learned about in this book. What parts of the filmmaking process were the most interesting to you? What do you notice now that you didn't before? How does the camera move? What props do you see? What colors pop on the screen? What sounds do you hear?

The most important thing to know the next time you watch a movie is that, whatever you're seeing or hearing or feeling, there's a good chance that the person behind it was a woman. That means that if you want, you can do it, too.

And that's a wrap!

ACKNOWLEDGMENTS

FIRST AND FOREMOST, I WANT TO THANK ALL THE WOMEN WHO inspired this book and took the time to talk to me for it. My favorite thing about working in the film industry is all the amazing friendships with absolutely fantastic female colleagues. You motivate and inspire me each and every day. Your creativity, perseverance, and love of your craft is such a joy to watch.

I must give extra thanks to Brea Grant, who was my very first interview for this book, and whose wisdom gave me a metric ton of guidance along the way. You are a wonder and I feel so lucky to be your friend.

So much love to Frank Woodward, who, many years ago now, took a very anxious young woman under his wing and taught her how to make movies and navigate the strange world of Los Angeles. Same goes to Sultan Saeed al Darmaki and Adam Cultraro. May we all someday make that giant seagull movie.

Of course, my editor, Britny, for your immediate enthusiasm for this book and for really getting what it meant to me. It started out as something so different and became something so much better. Frances, thank you for making it look so dang good! Thank you to the whole Running Press team for all your work on this.

Jen, you art queen. I couldn't ask for a better collaborator. Thank you, thank you, thank you for responding with instant excitement and amazing ideas when I emailed you out of the blue to say, "I have this idea . . ."

Amy Bishop, my phenomenal agent, there isn't enough champagne in the world to thank you for getting this project across the finish line.

Lauren, my best friend, for keeping me sane throughout this entire endeavor. I honestly don't think I could be an author without you.

Jeremy, you are the most wonderful person in the world a weird author like me could fall in love with. I love you and your gigantic, brilliant writer brain. Thank you for the endless support and love.

Finally, thanks to all the filmmakers whose creations made me want to follow in their footsteps, particularly Peter Jackson, Fran Walsh, and Philippa Boyens. *The Lord of the Rings* changed my life when I was eleven years old and opened my eyes to the magic of making movies.

And of course, my personal patron saint, Milicent Patrick, for showing me that women belong in the world of film.

GLOSSARY

ADAPT: in regard to filmmaking, to create a screenplay from already existing media like a book

ADR MIXER: the person who mixes the automated dialogue replacement

AMBIENT SOUND: background noise

ARMORER: the person responsible for the weapons used on screen

ART DEPARTMENT: the team responsible for creating the parts of the overall look of a film

ART DIRECTOR: the person responsible for bringing the production designer's creative ideas to life and for managing the art department

ASSISTANT DIRECTOR: the person who handles the logistics of the set during production

AUDITION: a tryout via a short performance

AUDITION TAPE: a recording of an audition

AUTOMATED DIALOGUE REPLACEMENT (ADR): the process of rerecording an actor's dialogue

BACKGROUND ACTORS: an actor in a background role

BACKGROUND CASTING DIRECTOR: the person responsible for casting background actors

BACKGROUND ROLES: a nonspeaking role that provides atmosphere or ambience in a scene

BACK LOT: a place on a studio lot with buildings and outdoor spaces to shoot

BEST BOY/GIRL/PERSON: the person second-in-command to the key grip or key gaffer

BLIMP: a cover for a microphone to protect it from picking up the wind

BLOCK: to plan out how everyone and everything is going to move in a scene

BOOM MICROPHONE: a microphone at the end of a long pole

BOOM OPERATOR: the person responsible for the boom microphone

BOOM POLE: long pole attached to the boom microphone

BUDGET: how much money is being spent on a film

CALL SHEET: a document containing all the details of that day's film shoot

CAMERA OPERATOR: the person responsible for operating the camera and capturing the shots

CASTING DIRECTOR: the person responsible for finding the right actors for a film

CATERING: the team responsible for providing hot, sit-down meals for a film cast and crew

CGI (COMPUTER GENERATED IMAGERY): effects created by computers

CINEMATOGRAPHER: a director of photography who also operates the camera

COLOR CORRECTING: fixing the colors of the footage

COLOR GRADING: stylizing the colors of the footage

COLORIST: the person responsible for color work in post-production

COMPOSITING: digitally combining images

COMPOSITION: how everything is arranged in a frame

CONCEPT ART: visual art that conveys ideas

CONCEPT ARTIST: someone who makes concept art

CONTINUITY: principle of making sure that all details in a film are consistent from shot to shot and from scene to scene

COSTUME DESIGNER: the person responsible for designing a film's costumes

COWRITER: someone who is part of a screenwriting team

CRAFT SERVICES (CRAFTY): the team responsible for providing snacks and beverages to a film cast and crew

CREDITS: acknowledgments of contributions to the film

DAILIES: the raw, unedited footage captured each day

DIALOGUE: the lines the actors say

DIALOGUE EDITOR: the person who edits a film's dialogue

DIEGETIC SOUND: any sound happening in the world of the film, or a sound that a character in the movie could hear

DIGITAL IMAGING TECHNICIAN (DIT): the person who works with the DP to manage the digital image that the camera is capturing

DIGITAL SET EXTENSION: a computer-generated extension to a real-life set

DIRECTOR: the person responsible for the creative vision of a film

DIRECTOR OF PHOTOGRAPHY: the person responsible for filming a movie

DIRECTOR'S CUT: a director's preferred version of a movie

DOLLY: a wheeled cart that a camera gets mounted to

DOLLY GRIP: the grip who operates the dolly

DOLLY TRACK: a line of rails for moving a dolly on

DRIVERS: the people responsible for driving vehicles during a film production

DUBBING (LOOPING): rerecording dialogue

EDIT BAY (SUITE): the room where a film is edited

EDITOR (PICTURE EDITOR): the person responsible for cutting and assembling the film

END CRAWL (CLOSING CREDITS): a list of all the cast and crew involved in the making of a film

EXERTIONS: the sounds actors make in a scene when they are making a physical effort

EXTERIOR: in regard to a script, this means the scene happens outside

FIGHT COORDINATOR: the person who choreographs and helps direct combat sequences

FILM COMPOSER: the person responsible for creating the score

FILM HAIRSTYLIST: the person responsible for both designing all the hairstyles for a film's characters as well as styling on set while the movie is shooting

FINAL CUT (DIRECTOR'S CHOICE): final say on the final film edit

FINAL CUT (EDITING): the finished cut of a film approved by the director and producer

FINANCING: providing money for a movie

FINE CUT: a finalized cut of a film before it is approved by the producer and director

FIRST ASSEMBLY CUT: an editor's first cut of a film

FIRST ASSISTANT CAMERA: the person responsible for assisting the camera operator

FIRST CUT: an accepted rough cut of a film

FLATS: sheets of plywood mounted onto a wooden frame made to look like part of the scene

FOCUS PULLER: See first assistant camera

FOLEY: sound effects

FOLEY ARTIST: the person responsible for creating and recording sound effects

GAFFER: the person responsible for the lighting on set

GELS: transparent materials used to change the way a light looks

GOING OVER BUDGET: spending more than the budget allows for

GREEN SCREENS: green backdrops for filming that a computer artist can digitally remove and replace with something else

GREENSPERSON: the person responsible for all the greenery and plants in a film

GRIPS: technicians who are responsible for setting and taking down lighting or electrical equipment

HEADSHOTS: photographs of an actor

HERO PROPS AND WEAPONS: props and weapons made with enough detail to be used for close ups

INTERIOR: in regard to a script, this means the scene happens inside

IN THE CAN: finished

JUMP CUT: an abrupt transition in a movie

KEY GRIP: the person in charge of the grip crew

LAVALIER MICROPHONES (LAV MICS): small microphones that attach to an actor's body or costume

LEADS: the main characters in a movie

LICENSE: paying for the right to use music, art, or other creative works that belong to someone else

LINE PRODUCER: the person responsible for daily operations on a film production

LINES: an actor's dialogue in a scene

LOCATION MANAGER: the person responsible for finding and managing film locations

LOGGING: the process of watching and sorting the collected dailies from the film shoot

MAIN TITLE DESIGNER: the person who designs the title sequence and opening credits

MAKEUP ARTIST: the person responsible for creating makeup designs and applying them to the actors

MANUAL: done by hand

MATTE PAINTINGS: massive paintings used as backgrounds in film scenes

MECHANICAL: done by machine

MOTION CAPTURE (MO-CAP): the process of digitally capturing an actor's movements and pasting them onto a digital model

MUSIC EDITOR: the person responsible for editing the recording of the score and syncing it to the film

MUSIC SUPERVISOR: the person responsible for choosing and licensing sounds for a film

NON-DIEGETIC SOUND: any sound that doesn't happen in the world of the film

ON LOCATION: shooting a movie in a real-world setting

OPENING CREDITS: credits shown at the beginning that include the most important members of the film production

PERFORMANCE CAPTURE: motion capture that includes facial expressions

PERIOD MOVIE: a film taking place in a different time period, usually historical in nature

POST-PRODUCTION COORDINATOR: the person responsible for managing the administrative work of post-production

POST-PRODUCTION SUPERVISOR: the person responsible for overseeing the post-production process

PRACTICAL EFFECTS: real-life effects created in front of the camera

PRINCIPAL PHOTOGRAPHY: the production stage of filmmaking

PRODUCER: the person who oversees and manages a film production

PRODUCTION ACCOUNTANT: the person responsible for managing a film's budget

PRODUCTION ASSISTANT: the person responsible for assisting the production office with various tasks on a film

PRODUCTION BUYER: a person responsible for shopping for and buying needed supplies for a movie

PRODUCTION COORDINATOR: the person in the production office who manages administrative tasks

PRODUCTION DESIGNER: the person who coordinates the overall aesthetic of a movie

PROP: object used or held by actors during their performance

PROP FABRICATOR: the person responsible for making props

PROP MASTER: the person responsible for creating and managing props

PULL THE FOCUS: to adjust the camera so that the shot is clear and sharp

PYROTECHNICIAN: the person responsible for pyrotechnics

PYROTECHNICS: fire-related special effects that happen in front of the camera

RAW FOOTAGE: footage as it is captured on set with no changes or edits at all

RERECORDING MIXER (SOUND MIXER): the person responsible for mixing all the elements of post-production sound into one track

ROTOSCOPING: tracing footage of a real actor moving to use for animation

ROUGH CUT: the first cut of a movie after preliminary editing

SCORE: a piece of instrumental music composed specifically for the movie and performed by a live orchestra for recording

SCREENPLAY: the script of a movie, which includes dialogue and plot

SCREENWRITER: the person who writes the screenplay

SCRIPT BREAKDOWN: an analysis of a screenplay that separates the needed production elements into lists

SCRIPT SUPERVISOR: the person responsible for tracking the script during productions

SECOND ASSISTANT CAMERA: the first assistant camera's assistant and the person responsible for the clapper

SECOND ASSISTANT DIRECTOR: the first assistant director's assistant

SECOND SECOND ASSISTANT DIRECTOR: the second assistant director's assistant

SECOND UNIT: a second filmmaking crew used to film scenes at a second location

SECOND UNIT DIRECTOR: the director of the second filmmaking unit

SET: the location or enclosure where a movie is filmed

SET BUILDER: the person responsible for the construction of a set

SET COSTUMER: the person responsible for managing the costumes on set during a production

SET DECORATOR: the person responsible for getting background objects like furniture and decorations situated how the art director wants them

SET DRESSER: the person who arranges the set dressing

SET DRESSING: furniture, decorations, and other background objects in a scene

SET MEDIC: a registered nurse or a paramedic who is always on set and attends to any health issues

SET PAINTER: the person responsible for painting a set

SHOT LIST: a list of all the needed shots for each scene

SOUND ASSISTANT: a person responsible for helping the sound team

SOUND DESIGNER: the person who creates the ambient sound, also known as the sound editor

SOUND EFFECTS: sounds other than dialogue or music

SOUND MIXER (PRODUCTION): the person responsible for capturing a film's sound during production

SOUNDTRACK: songs chosen, licensed, and sometimes even recorded specifically for a film

SPECIAL EFFECTS MAKEUP ARTIST: the person responsible for creating special makeup effects and anything that is beyond traditional beauty makeup

SPECIAL EFFECTS SUPERVISOR: the person responsible for managing special effects during production, also known as the special effects coordinator

SPECIAL EFFECTS TECHNICIANS: the team responsible for creating special effects

STEADICAM: a specialized camera rig that is worn like a backpack and stabilizes the camera

STEADICAM OPERATOR: the person who operates the steadicam rig

STORYBOARD ARTIST: an artist who creates storyboards

STORYBOARDS: a sequence of drawings that represent planned shots for a film or television scene

STRIKE: take down

STUDIO: an entertainment or film company's privately owned facilities used for shooting movies

STUDIO LOT: a compound of office buildings and big indoor stages where movies and TV shows are made

STUNT: a difficult physical feat performed for a movie

STUNT COORDINATOR: the person responsible for coordinating and planning all the stunts

STUNT DOUBLE: a stunt performer made up to look like the actor they are performing the stunt for

STUNT PERFORMER: the person performing a stunt

STUNT RIGGER: the person responsible for designing the system of ropes, pulleys, and harnesses that make stunts happen

STUNT RIGGER COORDINATOR: the person responsible for managing the team of stunt riggers

SUPERVISING SOUND EDITOR (SOUND SUPERVISOR): the person who hires and manages the sound team

SUPPORTING ROLES: the minor characters in a movie

TECH SCOUT: a visit to a potential filming location to figure out the technical details of shooting there

THEME: the melodic subject of a musical piece

TITLE CARDS: full-screen images featuring text that credits the stars of the film and major crew members

TITLE SEQUENCE: a presentation of the title of a film

TRANSPORTATION COORDINATOR: the person responsible for all transportation during a film production

TRANSPORT CAPTAIN: the person responsible for transporting the cast and crew of a movie

VFX ARTIST: a digital artist who creates visual effects

VFX SUPERVISOR: the person leading the VFX team

VIDEO VILLAGE: an area where all the camera feeds are shown on video monitors, so the director, DP, and camera crew can see each shot

VISUAL EFFECTS (VFX): special effects created by computers after filming

WILD SOUND: sound that is recorded without being in sync with video footage

WRAP: finish

WRAP PARTY: a party for the cast and crew after the production wraps

RECOMMENDED FILMS MADE BY WOMEN

~~~~~~~~~~~~~~~

HERE'S A BUNCH OF GREAT MOVIES THAT WERE MADE BY WOMEN, IN all kinds of roles. Watch them for some inspiration on your filmmaking journey and record your thoughts about them here. There's blank space at the bottom to add more movies that you've seen!

☆☆☆☆☆   Little Women (2019) _____

☆☆☆☆☆   A Wrinkle in Time _____

☆☆☆☆☆   Pet Sematary (1989) [SCARY!] _____

☆☆☆☆☆   Bend It Like Beckham _____

☆☆☆☆☆   Wonder Woman _____

☆☆☆☆☆   Across the Universe _____

☆☆☆☆☆   Lady Bird _____

☆☆☆☆☆   A League of Their Own _____

☆☆☆☆☆   Daughters of the Dust _____

☆☆☆☆☆   Captain Marvel _____

☆☆☆☆☆   Black Panther _____

☆☆☆☆☆   Little _____

☆☆☆☆☆   Queen of Katwe _____

☆☆☆☆☆   Dumplin' _____

☆☆☆☆☆   Eternals _____

☆☆☆☆☆   The Miseducation of Cameron Post _____

☆☆☆☆☆   The One and Only Ivan _____

☆☆☆☆☆ Black Is King

☆☆☆☆☆ Emma (2020)

☆☆☆☆☆ Whip It!

☆☆☆☆☆ Whale Rider

☆☆☆☆☆ Marie Antoinette (2006)

☆☆☆☆☆ The Farewell

☆☆☆☆☆ Fast Color

☆☆☆☆☆ Knock Down the House

☆☆☆☆☆ The Sun Is Also a Star

☆☆☆☆☆ The Half of It

☆☆☆☆☆

☆☆☆☆☆

☆☆☆☆☆

☆☆☆☆☆

☆☆☆☆☆

☆☆☆☆☆

☆☆☆☆☆

☆☆☆☆☆

☆☆☆☆☆

☆☆☆☆☆

☆☆☆☆☆

☆☆☆☆☆

☆☆☆☆☆

☆☆☆☆☆

☆☆☆☆☆

☆☆☆☆☆ _____

☆☆☆☆☆ _____

☆☆☆☆☆ _____

☆☆☆☆☆ _____

☆☆☆☆☆ _____

☆☆☆☆☆ _____

☆☆☆☆☆ _____

☆☆☆☆☆ _____

☆☆☆☆☆ _____

☆☆☆☆☆ _____

☆☆☆☆☆ _____

☆☆☆☆☆ _____

☆☆☆☆☆ _____

☆☆☆☆☆ _____

☆☆☆☆☆ _____

☆☆☆☆☆ _____

☆☆☆☆☆ _____

☆☆☆☆☆ _____

☆☆☆☆☆ _____

☆☆☆☆☆ _____

☆☆☆☆☆ _____

☆☆☆☆☆ _____

☆☆☆☆☆ _____

☆☆☆☆☆ _____

RESOURCE LIST

BEFORE YOU MAKE YOUR OWN MOVIE, HERE ARE SOME GREAT resources to help you learn more. There are lots and lots of free programs online. Make sure you ask a teacher, parent, guardian, librarian, or older sibling to help with the research!

KIDS' FILMMAKING PROGRAMS

http://archive.pov.org/filmmakers/resources/youth-filmmaking-programs.php

www.intofilm.org/

www.girls-in-focus.com/

www.learnaboutfilm.com/

www.studentfilmmakers.com/

www.womensvoicesnow.org/girls-voices-now-youth-development-program

FOR SCREENWRITING:

www.celtx.com

FILMMAKING ADVICE FOR KIDS:

https://youtu.be/4a_UfDuiJY

https://youtu.be/9HP9laxiwsk

https://youtu.be/5KH9C2-F4Dc

https://youtu.be/5PFuNz_Ld9Q

APPS AND WEBSITES FOR MAKING MOVIES:

www.commonsense.org/education/articles/16-websites-and-apps-for
-making-videos-and-animation

https://vimeo.com/blog/category/video-school

WOMEN MAKE MOVIES:

www.wmm.com/

FOR DOCUMENTARIES:

https://browngirlsdocmafia.com/

ABOUT THE AUTHOR
AND ILLUSTRATOR

MALLORY O'MEARA is the award-winning and bestselling author of *The Lady from the Black Lagoon* and *Girly Drinks*. Every week, she cohosts the literary podcast *Reading Glasses*. She lives in the mountains near Los Angeles with her two cats, where she is working on her next nonfiction book.

JEN VAUGHN is a cartoonist and narrative designer for video games and tabletop role-playing games. Her past comics include *Goosebumps: Download and Die, Avery Fatbottom: Renaissance Fair Detective,* and more. Every other week, find Jen befriending monsters on the family-friendly podcast *d20 Dames,* and running Fiasco games on Roll20's Twitch channel. In her free time, she enjoys creating physical puzzles to befuddle her friends and working on her balcony garden with cat, Hemlock, like a good druid.